Bad to the Bone

Exploring the many Facets of Aggression and Violent Behavior

By
Kevin O'Hagan

A CIP catalogue record for this book is available from the British Library

Printed and bound in Great Britain.

ISBN 0 9538555 4 6

Printed in Oct 2001 (1st edition)

Printed by
New Breed Publishing
Po box 511
Dagenham
Essex RM9 5DN

New Breed Publishing
Po Box 511
Dagenham
Essex RM9 5DN

www.newbreedbooks.co.uk

books@newbreed.worldonline.co.uk

Dedication

To my wife Tina and my wonderful children, Thomas, Jacob and Lauren. Your love and support spurs me on every day to achieve.

Acknowledgements
As always to Tina for her patience to type up my scruffy notes.
To Jamie for being a true and supportive mate.
To my training buddies, Paul, Rob, Matt, Ross, Mark, Steve and the 'mob'
Dale at ML Sports Promotions for MMA action in the South West.
Scott for the 'move'. All the 'gang' for a memorable 40th.

CONTENTS

About the Author

Kevin O'Hagan is a veteran Martial Artist of nearly 30 years experience. In his time he has learnt many different arts and trained with just about every leading light in the fighting arts.

He is a 6th Dan black belt with a full masters degree in Combat Ju jutsu and is also a senior Self Protection coach. His deep knowledge and interest in practical and combat orientated technique also brought him to researching and experiencing the psychology side of violence and how the human mind functions and perceives aggression.

This fascination with the subject lead to this his fourth book for New Breed Publications. His previous books have dealt with the physical reality of violent confrontation and Self Defence; this latest book explores the mental side of preparing for aggression.

As well as a professional Martial Arts/Self Protection instructor, Kevin is a qualified fitness/sports coach and has recently started a conflict Management business called 'Safe and Sound Management U.K.

Other books by Kevin O'Hagan

I thought you'd be bigger, a small persons guide to fighting back
In you Face, Close quarter combat
Grappling with Reality, Survival on the floor.

Preface

When I decided to write this book, it dawned on me that I had devoted nearly 30 years to learning, training and teaching a multitude of nefarious fighting skills capable of inflicting great harm on another human being.

It may sound highly dramatic but I had the skill and knew how to kill!

A frightening and sober thought. But the more I have trained and developed my technique the less and less I am inclined to use it and would try to avoid violent confrontation like the plague.

This year I became 40 years of age and they say with age comes wisdom. I don't know about this but I feel you begin to see things in a different light.

When I first started Martial Arts training as a 14 year old school boy of slight build, below average height and lacking confidence in his ability to defend himself, I craved for the physical skills to be able to beat up my would be aggressors. I felt that by having these skills that it would get rid of all my self-doubt and fears.

I took to training with a passion that has stayed with me ever since. Through those years I've become fitter, stronger and conditioned. I developed good fighting skills and newfound confidence. Martial Arts really began to change my life.

Achieving a 6th Dan black belt in Ju Jutsu was a proud moment for me. It was a milestone in my Martial Arts career where I had achieved much.

I also hold black belts in two other Martial Arts and am also a qualified Self Protection Coach. I had competed in the fighting arena and achieved medals and trophies, last competing at 39 years of age!

Becoming a fitness coach and earning diplomas in sports coaching and sports psychology and writing three self defence books were great achievements for me as I had left school with very few qualifications.

My Martial Arts skills have helped me produce a series of video training tapes and gain recognition on television and radio.

I became obsessed and fanatical with physical training. I put myself and my students through some brutal workouts!

Along with my Martial Arts training I learnt to box, wrestle and cross train in limited rules mixed Martial Arts competition.

A few years ago I began to realise that I had pushed myself to the limits of physical skills and that I had tried and tested myself in every possible arena and the 'buzz' of being involved in the physical contact wasn't as strong or appealing anymore.

I began to develop more and more interest in the psychological side of why violence starts, the type of people that perpetrates it and what makes them tick.

When I was younger I only wanted the physical answer to Self Defence and tended to believe the answer was in your fists, where now I know 90% is using the brain, the strongest of all our human weapons.

Being able to physically look after yourself is only part of the picture, having a deeper understanding of how we view violence, analysing how situations occur and examining our own perceptions of danger and fear can go a long way to making us mentally stronger.

I don't profess to be a 'Master' of Martial Arts or a professor of psychology but what I have learnt over my long journey has been through first hand experience not some text book theory.

I have made a lifetime study of fighting arts, fighters, violence, aggression and have come to many conclusions that I would like to share in the hope it will give you, the reader a better understanding in a shorter span of time than in my own experience.

At this stage in my life I feel I have found the right balance where I no longer fear violence but I have a healthy respect for it and will do everything to avoid it unless I am left with absolutely no other choice. My outlook is different these days. I feel stronger physically and mentally now at 40 than I ever did at 25. Looking back I still had a lot to learn in those days but at the time didn't see it.

My good friend and Self Protection pioneer Geoff Thompson is fond of quoting from the excellent book, 'The Art of War' by

Sun Tzu. One of his favourites that sums up how I feel and the theme of this book is as follows. 'Understand yourself and understand your enemy and you need not fear the result of a 100 battles'

I feel I finally understand this profound statement after a long hard voyage.

Kevin O'Hagan Feb. 2001
'Forty is the old age of youth' 'Fifty is the youth of old age'

Introduction

The annals of history are stained with the blood of violence. Since man was created he has waged war against his fellow man on a large or small scale. It just seems that there is something in our make-up that makes us want to perpetrate violence against others.

Man is the only species on the planet that kills for pleasure. In the animal kingdom they only kill for food or survival, it is nature's way.

We as humans marvel and shudder at the power and ferocity of a lion bringing down a zebra or a great white shark attacking a seal. We comment on how savage the acts are, but don't realise that humans have done far worse things to fellow human beings (and indeed animals).

The atrocities of war, the horrors of torture, rape, child abuse and the abhorrent crimes of serial killers make the survival instincts of the animal world some what tame.

But we tend to feel we are civilised and because we are the most intelligent race in existence, we can be excused in some way for our violent acts.

It's a sad fact of life that our acts of violence are a reoccurring procedure, which seems to get worse and worse as time goes by.

Not a week goes by when we don't read in the national or local newspapers about some heinous crime or act of wanton violence. Television news will report such incidents on a regular basis or friend, colleague or neighbour will relate to you some episode.

Wrong as it may seem we tend to take all this in our stride, simply because it is everyday occurrences. It no longer holds the shock impact as it used to.

I personally still get sickened and angry about these crimes of violence but it no longer surprises or shocks me.

I have grown to realise that man is just about capable of anything. There is no stone un-turned, no taboos!

Violence and the horrors it brings is unfortunately at this present time is here to stay. It is not going to go away and nobody is immune to it. Remember you could be a victim of it, today, tomorrow, next week? Who knows? We had better accept this fact and do all we can to minimise the threat.

Today's society is one of pressure and stress. Everybody seems to be rushing, with no time for anybody else.

Heavy workloads, schedules and business targets have all got to be dealt with and the stress gets higher.

Aggression is everywhere we go. Aggressive salesman, aggressive drivers, aggressive shoppers, aggressive workers, aggressive children and so on and so on. It just seems sometimes to be spiralling out of control.

Nobody appears to have a decent word to say about others or have time to care or help. Society dictates me, me, me and the I want, must have syndrome. All this makes us more aggressive and feel we should be in the front of the queue and that we won't wait, we won't be 'fobbed' off. We want it all!!

Sometimes on my working travels I have seen examples of humans being at their worst. Selfish, greedy, rude, borish and aggressive. It can begin to make you doubt today's social structures.

Now don't get me wrong I have long ago done a character x-ray of myself and examined where I was going wrong and recognised the foolish, stupid and wrong things I have done in my life and started to readdress the balance, which I still strive for everyday.

But when I see one act of kindness or care by another or if I can do that act myself, it restores all your faith and allows a little light into your life, otherwise we are in danger of being immersed in the dark side. When this happens we are in danger of becoming involved in the dark side too.

On a wide scale there isn't too much we can do about world violence but on a personal level there is and we must work to battle it.

In the following chapters we will look at how we have grown up to be programmed in certain beliefs about violent crime and although the average person can be pretty clued up on today's trends and fades, they can still be pretty naive or living in the past when it concerns the subject of violence and self protection.

Other chapters will explore our fears and beliefs on the subject, the perpetrators violence, the facts and the myths and the psychology of what makes them tick and how we can identify the danger signs of the human predator and not become a victim. Hopefully by the end of this book you will be more aware and prepared to face the dangers of modern society.

'And this is the condemnation.' 'That light has come into the world and man loved darkness rather than light because their deeds were evil.' John 3:19

Chapter 1
Beware the bully

If you were Lucky enough, like myself, to have grown up in a good and stable family existence with the protection of loving parents, you will have found your very early childhood years quite trouble free.

The comfort and security you got from your parents kept you safe and they tried to shield you from any harm or danger.

My real first inkling that life wasn't all sweetness and light was when I first stepped out into the big wide world on my first day at school.

At school you quickly established good friends but at the same time your path crossed with the 'not so nice' kid, the bully in his or her fledgling state!

Suddenly the comfort zone of your world is upset whenever you encountered the 'bully'. You begin to realise that the stories that your parents may have read you that included evil characters were not just fairytales; they actually exist in one shape or another.

Early encounters with the bully or aggressive child can shape how you view people for the rest of your life.

Although I can say I was never a regular victim of bullying. I had my fair share of encounters to make me still despise bullies and bullying behaviour even today.

I used to dread running into these type of people as basically they ruined your day. You could be having a good time, getting on alright with your lessons, looking forward to a dinner time break and suddenly 'bang', there they are like the proverbial bad penny and you get that sinking feeling in your stomach.

They would start asking you a series of personal and blunt questions, or they would insult you about your looks, clothes, the way you spoke. This could progress to taking under intimidation your personal belongings. This may be items like a pen, pencil or ruler, working up to your lunch or any money you had on your person.

So from a child bullying you for a chair or a cloakroom peg or for a kick of a football it would progress, as they get older, into more serious things.

Of course if I mentioned this to my parents they would give me sound advice. Don't let them take anything off of you, stand up to them and don't be pushed around. Like I said good advice but what I wanted to know is how?

This aspect can be a child's stumbling block. They know what they ought to do, but actually putting it into practice is a different thing altogether.

It is not in some children's nature to be aggressive or should I say assertive, they struggle with it greatly. No matter what you tell them they just cannot bring themselves to stand up for themselves.

For those who are assertive they can't see the problem, but for those who lack this, it is a major issue and one that can affect them through into adulthood.

It's like a vicious circle. They don't want to stand up to the bully mainly because of consequences. I have my own children and I have taught Martial Arts to children for many years. When I have posed them the question of standing up to bullying, many have stated they were frightened if they became assertive that they would escalate the situation and be physically hit.

The other answer was they were worried about what happens after when the teachers, headmaster, parents etc get involved and you are in trouble for fighting.

These issues although addressed from a child's perspective can also be issues for adults when confronted by an aggressive individual.

Sometimes adults I have trained in my classes will say when they have been confronted by hostile antagonist that it felt just like going back to the school yard and that they had experienced great feelings of helplessness and felt like they wanted the security and comfort of their mum.

The body does act in some strange ways under extreme stress and a lot of our infantile traits begin to surface, even though you thought you had buried them away with your toys forever.

As you progress from Primary school to Secondary School the step can be quite a large one in most respects. You may be the 'big fish' at the end of your Primary School days but you then become the 'small fish' once again, when you go to Secondary School.

The confidence and assurance you achieved in your last term at the 'little school' now takes a bit of a battering as you move up a 'league'. This again can be felt in many aspects of our life when we move out of our 'comfort zones'

I have witnessed many people supremely confident in one aspect of their lives but when change comes beckoning they panic and fall apart. We are all guilty of building comfort zones or perimeters we like to stay in. Some people stay in them all their lives and never step outside their safe zone or never look to see what is on the other side of the hill. What a waste of lives opportunities.

Anyway, back to Secondary School, intimidation and bullying also goes up a league and the Primary School name-calling or 'Mickey taking' seems quite harmless in comparison to the next levels.

When you are very young you have the capacity to forgive and forget quite easily. As I like to say infants don't hold grudges. You can scold a youngster and they can be upset and in the next instant they are asking you to play with them, the incident totally forgotten.

I can remember as a youngster encountering a bully and having a bad time, then I0 minutes later I was kicking a football around with my mates, the incident pushed to the back of my mind. Our brains have the ability to do this. Of course the respite of confrontation may be only short lived until it surfaces it's ugly head again.

When you become a teenager though things are different. You take things more to heart. You get upset about callous remarks and confrontation it can play upon your mind and incessant bullying can then effect the whole structure of your life. Indeed some teenagers have committed suicide over the misery they have felt through bullying. A terrible and tragic scenario.

The trend in teenage circles now at present is to have groups of kids who bully rather than the stereotype singular person. The gang mentality is worse, one feeding off another. All jostling for recognition and acceptance from their friends. One will 'egg' another on and soon we have a 'feeding frenzy' like a group of sharks.

Girls and boys alike will go around in groups to bully and this can be a lot more intimidating than just one person.

I have found though with every group there is always one person leading and controlling the others with may be a 'lieutenant' for back up. The rest are pretty insignificant and are 'hangers on', they hoping to gain respect and belonging.

If you deal with the 'leader' you control them all. None of them will make a move without the leaders say so. They are all basically cowards.

One thing though that may change this balance is the presence of alcohol or drugs.

Unfortunately in modern times a considerable number of teenagers will be experimenting with both and this can make them unpredictable and dangerous.

Many recorded incidents show that what started off as general intimidation ended up in brutal violence resulting in some instances with tragic and fatal results.

I recall on many occasions being chased by groups of youths, shouting and screaming like a rabid pack of dogs! It's not a pleasant situation to be in and you suddenly find out you can break the 4 minute mile with no problem!

I relate here an incident that at the time wasn't funny but later I looked back on it and managed to have a chuckle.

When I was about I5/I6 years old, a group of us used to go to a youth club on the other side of my hometown of Bristol.

(Remember youth clubs where have they gone?) We were all at the time staunch Bristol Rovers supporters, yet this Youth club was in Bristol City territory. Anyway the word went around that we were Rovers supporters and we got chased by a large group of City fans. At one stage myself and my good friend Shaun were doing a great impression of Linford Christie (minus the lunchboxes) and we glanced back to see the younger brother of another mate just about to be caught by the coat collar and dragged down. The scene reminded me of those wild life documentaries when a pride of lions give chase to a group of gazelles. They get a younger and slower one separated from the herd and move in for the kill!

Well, Shaun and me looked back exchanging glances as if to say 'do we stop running and help or keep going?' The problem is under severe conditions your mind and legs don't always work together! Anyway without a word of a lie, from one brief instance of seeing this young lad ready to 'go under', in the next breath he had over taken us both! He must have had an extra burst of adrenalin that had spurred him on from a certain beating. It's amazing what the body can do under stress!

I can recall many teenage episodes of confrontation quite clearly. It's amazing how the brain has the ability to remember vividly bad things in your life and how good images can fade so quickly.

I can replay scenarios in my mind some 25 years ago quite accurately and still experience the feelings I had at that stage of my life. Looking back in retrospect a lot of the situations I could of handled and stood up to some of these bullies, but again the little matter of consequences or after math prevented me.

I feel even without my later Martial Arts training I could have put up a pretty reasonable showing if it got physical but instead I let myself be intimidated. In later years in my 20's I looked back on these incidents with bitter regret and envisaged how I would have handled them with my new found Martial Arts skills. I visualised pounding their sneering faces to a pulp and would see them bleeding on the floor pleading with me to stop.

I hated myself for not having done it but now I realise that you learn with experience you don't know at 16 years of age what you will know at 25 and you don't know at 25 what you will know at 40!

But having said that I do feel greatly for kids caught up in these situations where they feel helpless to stand up to a bully. It is a terrible feeling and one that I wouldn't wish on my kids or any others.

We have to be realistic though, it goes on and you have got to educate your child on the situations, so they can be prepared. Avoiding the bully is good advice but in places like a school it is not always possible and inevitable your paths will cross.

I often wonder where those bullies of yesteryear have gone. Are they still carrying on their traits? Are they now bullying husbands, wives, bosses? Or did somebody sort them out, did they meet a bigger and stronger adversary that showed them the error of their ways?

Remember the bully thrives on your fear; this is what fuels them to keep pursuing you. You unfortunately cannot avoid the bully forever, somewhere you are going to have to stand up to them otherwise you will be running scared the rest of your life.

Nobody wants to live their life in fear of confrontation. It is not healthy for the body or mind to be in a constant state of anxiety.

When I was aged about 12 or 13, in my street where I lived there was a family that had a reputation for trouble. There were 4 or 5 boys in this family and all were troublemakers.

If they were hanging around outside their house when I left mine, I would spot them and head up the road instead of down. It may have been a longer route for my journey but it saved me the inevitable confrontation.

Now this is a great tactic anyway and I still teach this principle in my self protection classes. Why put yourself at risk when there is another option. I still use this survival option even now. The difference being now I am not running scared, I just don't want the hassle of the confrontation. I want to live a stress free and trouble free life, the best I can.

Back then I was avoiding because I was frightened and it's a feeling I didn't enjoy. I used to concoct elaborate plans of avoidance and have many escape routes mapped out. Infact I became quite an expert at this and it stood me in good stead for later on in life.

But sometimes you didn't always get it right. I suppose the naivety of such a young age gave you a false sense of security.

If I left my house and the street was clear I would walk down it on red alert as I neared this family's house. When I passed it without incident I would breath a great sigh of relief and relax somewhat. That was usually when I would walk around the corner at the end of the street and bump right into them!

You see at that time my immaturity only recognised the problem being associated with my street and their house. I didn't have the foresight to know I could bump into these guys anywhere, anytime. What I am trying to say is you cannot run scared all your life because bullies are everywhere in many guises and they are unfortunately part of our life and most certainly the growing up process.

These early childhood recollections bring the reality of society home to you and let you know that when you step out into the 'big bad world' your mum, dad, older brother or sister will not be there to hold your hand. You have got to learn to deal with these problems, the majority of times on your own.

As you get older you may get more assertive and confident, but make sure this is not just a flimsy front because the bullies and street predators will see through the facade. They will know that under the bravado, that you are still a victim. If you are going to play the assertive role make sure it is totally convincing. You must plant the seed of uncertainty in the bully's mind. This will make them unsure of you and they may not want to step over the line to see if you are the 'genuine article' or not!

Remember a bully doesn't want to fight you, he wants to beat you up and have done. This can be either verbally or physically.

It takes a really strong character to stand up and be assertive on a regular basis.

I found even after taking up Martial Arts training, I still struggled with self-doubt. Sometimes I felt strong and positive in a potentially dangerous situation, other times I felt weak and negative and just wanted to be somewhere else.

After many many years of training I realised these were natural feelings and that my body was reacting to aggression in its normal way. I had to train my mind to understand these feelings before I could hope to control them.

It certainly isn't easy to do and you will continually have to battle the negative thoughts and feelings, just like the bullies.

I have found when things are going well and you feel at your best your mind has a nasty habit of inventing a problem or worry, that isn't really there. When this happens you must swipe it aside and be assertive and gain control otherwise it can niggle and niggle away and destroy your confidence.

Try not to forget that confrontation may be just around the next corner and you may have to deal with it the next time you step out of your door.

Many children think once I leave school I will leave the bullies behind with it, but that is not the case. You will find bullying is not all about being 'in your face' and snarling and spitting threats. Adults can bully in different and more subtle ways by using manipulation, blackmail, guile and sublime threat and intimidation. Some people seem to roam into one bad relationship, marriage or job after another and carry on being bullied in one shape or form for the rest of their lives.

Don't let it be you, you must change the way you feel and strive to become a stronger person.

I have learnt through experience not to run scared. This doesn't mean you have to follow my path and gain my 'truth' through the Martial Arts. You may find a different path, as long as it gets the same results in the end, it doesn't matter.

Chapter 2
Fantasy world of violence

'We live in a fantasy world, a world of illusion. The great task of life is to find reality.' Iris Murdoch - The Times, 15th April 1983

Growing up in the late 60's and 70's I was a fanatical reader of the Marvel Super hero comics. Great characters like the Hulk, Spiderman, Captain America and many others captured my young imagination.

I longed to be like the hero's of those comic books. I wanted to be strong, brave and fearless. I wanted to be in control of all my enemies and be able to battle for righteousness and justice as I deemed it in my eyes.

I lost myself in these books for many years and found them a great comfort in times of uncertainty or insecurity. I often dreamt about obtaining super powers and surprising a person I didn't like when they picked on me by unleashing my mighty skills! Of course it was all childish fantasy, make-believe and deep down I knew it could never be and that my comic book hero's didn't really exist. But when you are growing up you all need hero's to look up to and model yourself on and doesn't this go on far beyond your childhood years?

The 70's for me were full of different hero's in one shape or form and at one time or another myself and my mates believed we were these people in make believe games. Here is a small list of such hero's, just to jog the memory.

Batman, Superman, Six Million Dollar Man, James Bond, The Professionals, Clint Eastwood, Charles Bronson, Arthur of the Britons, Starsky and Hutch, Bruce Lee and the list goes on and on. This all goes on through other stages of your life as you begin to get older and start moulding your personality. I remember avidly watching Sylvester Stallone in Rocky and Rambo movies loving every second of them, as to Chuck Norris and Arnold Schwarzenegger. These were the heros of my 20's and I used to try hard to emulate them.

Looking back now I must have been a right 'plonker' at times but I suppose it's part of growing up.

I feel though that whatever age you are we all like that brief moment of escapism. Where we can visualise we are that screen hero.

I have been in cinemas where I have watched Rocky films or Clint Eastwood's 'Dirty Harry' movies and seen men of all ages stand up and cheer when said character have won an encounter with rival boxers or criminals. It's contagious and I defy any male around my age not to get a tingle down the spine when they see Stallone in training as Rocky and hear the adrenalin pumping theme tune. Or stop a small grin playing on their lips when they hear Eastwood say those immortal words, 'Go ahead punk make my day!'

We all love it, the triumph of good over evil; the hero wins against all odds. How many thousand books, films and TV shows have been built around those themes?

Maybe a lot of people enjoy this fantasy world of violence because they know deep down the real world isn't quite like it and they haven't got the strength of their screen hero's to defeat their enemies. I certainly felt like this at one stage of my life.

A problem can start to develop when people can't distinguish between the two and the fantasy world laps over into the real. There are many 'loose cannons' strutting around our streets lost individuals that sometimes can progress to becoming potential killers. (more about this later).

On a lesser scale these people play out their hero's traits and copy their actions. Today with a deluge of Gangster Rap and similar, a lot of teenagers are strutting around like hardened American criminals. In the pubs and clubs there are a fair share of 40-year-old adolescents behaving like 'bad guys', who should know better.

Watch out for these people and don't assume it's all bluff and posing. Some are deadly serious about the image and will go to any lengths to prove it.

On the other side of the coin we have the naivety of some people who think that the violence that happens on our screens only happens in the world of cinema.

They just can't see the dangers in the real world. They have this 'that couldn't possibly happen', attitude that will make them a victim. Sure there is a lot of extreme and over the top violence in the film world but some of it can be a pretty accurate portrayal.

Forget the Van Damme rubbish but some TV films can be quite hard hitting and it is hammering home the fact that violence of this nature does exist and happens on our streets and in our society everyday.

We have got to make sure we realise this but where the actors can get up and walk away after one of these brutal scenes, in real life you may not be able to do so.

Make no mistake, however realistic the fantasy world tries to portray violence it is never quite like the real thing.

When reality knocks on the door it is the worst of feelings and your never quite prepared, no matter what you may think.

It's like watching, 'Casualty' or 'ER' and believing you are ready to confront a road traffic accident. It's worlds apart when it's real and you witness first hand horrific injury and trauma.

I have been a qualified First Aider for ten years or more and passed the exams and test each time with flying colours but the classroom practise, know matter how good can't prepare you wholly for the real thing. On many occasions I have had to use my first aid skills in real life and it's always a lot harder when confronted by flowing blood, broken bones or unconsciousness.

Real life violence is the same. It is scary and it's the last place you want to be.

You can watch hundreds of boxing matches for instance on television and in the sterile and desensitised environment it doesn't seem real. Sit in the front row of a boxing match and actually hear the leather of the gloves pounding on muscle and bone! See the spray of sweat and blood. Hear the grunts and groans of the fighters and feel their pain and it's oh so different to the 'rasamataz' of the TV spectacle.

It's the same with the 'armchair critic' who curses and complains about a 'fighter' calling them useless or rubbish. My answer to these people is don't knock it till you've tried it!

There's a world of difference between thinking you can box and actually putting on a pair of gloves and giving it a try. A big difference. I speak from experience!

Where the fantasy world of book and film depicts 'fighting' as something romantic and awe-inspiring, 'real fighting' is anything but!

Remember back to a schoolyard brawl you may have experienced as a child. If you didn't enjoy the 'experience then, believe me you aren't going to relish it when your all grown up!

A lot of Martial Artists are guilty of look at 'fighting' through rose coloured glasses and visualise themselves performing spinning heel hook kicks and jumping side kicks to defend themselves on the streets. I admit as a young man so did I, until the first 'real' situation drops on your doorstep and you realise the fancy stuff doesn't work outside the Dojo (training hall). Yet many instructors carry on teaching out-dated and woefully inappropriate or ineffective technique to their students.

As I always say show me your best Martial Arts skills when you are crammed up against the inside of a telephone box with a mugger sticking a knife under your chin! This scenario is more in line with 'reality' than exchanging punches, blocks and kicks.

It's not just Martial Artists. We also have the would be 'fighters' that have learnt their deadly fighting skills from watching every Van Damme movie! They really believe they are killers. These people would have a job to fight a cold.

The other category is the people that 'bury their heads in the sand' and deny that brutal violence exists in their neighbourhood and if it does it happens to 'Joe Bloggs', not them. This is an extremely dangerous attitude of mind to live with.

These people who believe that danger doesn't exist, cannot possibly see the early warning signs of a situation and will not be able to evaluate and avoid. After all if you don't expect something to happen how can you hope to avoid it.

One of the foremost instructors of Self Protection in the UK, is Peter Consterdine. In his excellent book 'Streetwise (Protection Publications) he constantly mentions that people well versed in personal security methods will still fall foul to attack because they lack expectancy and acceptance that they could be a victim. I found this a major key factor in teaching people good Self Protection. Some of us must get out of the fantasy realm and see the world, how it is, there are some very bad people in it who prey on the innocent. You must accept no matter who you are or what your experience or abilities, maybe you can be a victim if you walk around in a 'victim state', i.e. switched off in denial that it can happen.

The comic and film world of fantasy needs to stay where it is, do not draw your experience of Self Protection or 'fighting' skills from these sources otherwise you will be sorely disappointed.

'Imagination and fiction make up more than 3/4 of our real life'

Simon Weil: Gravity and Grace

Chapter 3
'Who's bad'

'Do you know my record, Callaghan' 'Yeah, you're a legend in your own mind! Clint Eastwood - Sudden Impact

In answer to the above statement, I would say just about everybody in this high pressure and aggressive modern society is clamouring to make the claim that they are 'BAD'. In the Martial Arts world, sport, music, TV and films we are daily informed about the 'hard men', tough guys and 'Hell raisers'. Guys you wouldn't want to cross or argue with, monsters that you just don't tangle with unless you have some sort of 'deathwise'.

The press and media are responsible for programming our minds about these characters and making us believe everything we hear about them are true. Also these said people get carried away on the tide of stories and start believing it to and go out of their way on any given opportunity to fuel the images of the 'badass'

Think for a moment about sporting names like Vinnie Jones, Brian Moore, Ronnie O'Sullivan, Mike Tyson and many more have all been labelled with the tags of hardmen, hellraisers and tough guys. Rightly or wrongly? Who am I to judge? Music? Liam Gallagher, a supposed 'bad boy', likewise Mark Morrison, Puff Daddy, and Eminiem. Television gives us many tough guys in soaps and dramas, some said to be just like their screen characters, the same can be said for the film world, there is an endless list of self proclaimed badmen and hardnuts!

Martial Arts, in recent times because of the big interest in NHB fighting and its like, are reporting all the time on people claiming to be the 'Toughest Man on the Planet' - a hell of a claim to make, but they're out there believing the hype.

People are becoming obsessed with these tales and are being force-fed information through book, magazine, video and computer to add fuel to the fire and rocket some individuals into the heady heights of notoriety.

In the Martial Arts world today the assumption seems to be if you are not a bare knuckled fighter, NHB competitor, doorman, bodyguard or Super Ninja Turtle then you ain't nothing! 25, 30,

40 years of training in the Martial Arts seems to hold nothing to someone who has cracked a few drunks' heads 'on the door', these people are elevated to a pedestal of reverence and awe.

Now don't get me wrong: I have promoted and endorsed realistic training, cross training and self protection and I have utmost respect for truly class instructors who have had a 'door' background, like my friends and fellow martial artists Geoff Thompson, Peter Consterdine, Jamie O'Keefe, Dave Briggs amongst others. But there are many more individuals out there who have jumped on the band-wagon and are doing the Martial Arts more harm than good with their self proclaimed 'war' stories and boasts of their 'ass kicking' prowess. There are guys who are suddenly masters of all these arts Boxing, Karate, Judo, Sambo, Vale Tudo, JKD, Savate, Taekwondo, Thai, Ju Jutsu, Self Protection -who have also been; doormen, bodyguards, ex-army, security! They have done the lot and they're still only 25 years old, amazing!

Where are they all coming from? One trying to out do another in the 'heavy geezer' stories!

As stated, I love realistic training. I have written articles and books on the subjects and still teach those principles but I personally have never claimed to be a 'tough guy' or 'super' Kung Fu 'killer' I have trained bloody hard in Martial Arts for 30 years and devoted a big chunk of my life to it. Those who know me know my abilities and my passion for teaching and training. I can perform under pressure and have put myself on the line, but what I also try to keep in my art is humility, respect and discipline. I don't have to strut around all the time trying to convince others of my abilities.

My worry is these aspects of training will disappear totally from modern Martial Arts. I feel it's down to myself and fellow instructors to ensure that together with promoting and teaching realistic training we also promote humility, respect and discipline, otherwise the arts will be in danger of deteriorating into just a brawl.

People who do not really know me or others like Geoff Thompson, Jamie O'Keefe, Dave Briggs, Alan Charlton etc have the opinion that we are all just head butt ' em, bite 'em and knock them out merchants, nothing could be further from the truth! We have all had extensive Martial Arts training and all come by one route or another from a more traditional background. We are just all realists who have strived to take our training into the millennium. I must stress also that these men have never made the claim of being 'tough guys' yet they most certainly could adopt that title if they wished, they are the genuine articles amongst so many others who are not but who believe they are!

So where do all the stories, tales and reputations build from? Outside of the areas I mentioned every town, city, neighbourhood, street and pub, have their own self-proclaimed 'hard men', where does it all originate from?

Let's go back to school days. You have just left primary school where in your last year you were a 'big fish' in a little pond. Now at secondary school the roles have again reversed. In your first dinner break your best mate, whose brother has already been at secondary school for a few years, takes you for a guided tour of the playgrounds, filling you in on all the essential things you will need to know to survive the trauma of the 'big school!' He points out to you: 'Look see that kid, he's the hardest kid in the school, A right animal, even the teachers are frightened of him'. You look at this seemingly giant of a lad who has already grown in size due to the story you have just heard. You stare in awe, a mixture of fear and respect come over you.

Next you are shown a lesser mortal. 'The hardest kid in your year'. That's Joe Bloggs, right nutter he is, punched a teacher last year and threatened him with a flick knife, you want to stay clear of him, you're told! You glance at the 'nutter', wary that you don't catch his eye (you can always give it back!) and walk on.

'Here's the school psycho' (is his name Norman Bates?), you're informed. Burnt down the gym in his last school, he was expelled. His brother is inside doing time for GBH, I wouldn't mess with him.'

There it is, from an early age the stage has been set. You have taken everything as the gospel truth and you don't question it. In a few years time you'll be telling the same stories to somebody else only they will have got slightly taller. A bit gets added on for extra effect and 'psycho' has now burnt down the whole school and not just the gym! It goes on when you go to work, there's always somebody out to prove that you don't mess with them. There is always some story, some claim, some reputation.

The local pubs are the same, each with their own 'bad ass'. 'Don't sit on that chair mate, that's 'Big Harry's' and so it continues.'

Some live with the fears and beliefs of others because they are told to; they allow themselves to be brain washed.

Now there are undoubtedly some 'tough guys' out there who can handle and back up their reputations. I have known a few in my time, most though are not what you might expect. Remember: having a shaven skull, a body covered in tattoos and every orifice pierced doesn't mean you're 'hard'. Pumping weights every day and walking around in a 'muscle vest' - like you are carrying two rolls of carpet under your arms - doesn't make you a tough guy.

We are again conditioned by what we perceive or are programmed to perceive. Don't mess with him he's a doorman, boxer, ex-con, bodyguard, biker, skinhead, para, black belt, Morris dancer (no, last one's not right!) You see what I mean, we immediately assume these people are dangerous. Some are, the majority not.

Do we ever hear the claim 'don't mess with him he's a doctor, law student, psychologist, builder!' No, of course we don't. Yet some of the world's most notorious serial killers were exactly that! It's back to what we are programmed to believe. Rapists and murders do not lurk in the woods, wearing a hockey mask and brandishing a machete. One of America's worst serial killers, Ted Bundy was a handsome, articulate and well-mannered ex-college student. The last person you would expect to rape, bludgeon and hack to death 35 plus victims! You cannot judge a book by its cover!

Reputations can be manufactured and moulded to suit people's needs. I remember Geoff Thompson talking in one of his seminars about a guy in Coventry who bit off another man's ear in a fight. I believe this was some 10 years ago and he's never had a fight again due to the massive reputation he received. People still treat him with reverence and give him a wide berth.

Some reputations stay with you for life, for example the Krays. At one time their reputations were essential to them, in the end they probably became their undoing, as the laws of the land deemed them still unfit to be released from prison after 30 years and eventually was the death of them.

In recent times I have read the autobiographies of Lenny 'The Guv'nor' Mc Lean and Roy 'Pretty Boy' Shaw, without question two genuine tough nuts with awesome, reputations, who could definitely walk the walk and talk the talk! Yet in their books both give different accounts of their unlicensed meetings in the ring, with many conflicting and hugely contradictory points. Who's right? Who's wrong? Both had massive reputations to uphold. Shaw once dubbed the 'Hardest man in London' McLean 'The Guv'nor of the bare knuckled fighting scene.' I don't suppose we will ever fully know the truth.

Reputations can be a great asset or a big hindrance. It's as much a burden to carry one as it is a benefit. Rickson Gracie has been dubbed 'the best fighter on the planet'. I hasten to say I have not heard that he has said this but even so that is a hell of a claim to live up to. OK, maybe when you're in your prime but what about when you're past it?

It's like the 'fastest gun in the West'. There will always be somebody younger and quicker around the corner waiting to take your title, that's life, no matter how good you think you are! There are some who will take it by fair means or foul. If you carry the 'rep' as a hardman you have to live with that 24 hours a day. You will not be able to disregard it at any given time because others won't allow it. When you are out with your wife or kids, when you are visiting your elderly mum, when you are sunning yourself in foreign parts, there will always be somebody looking for a 'shot at the crown. It is a hard life to lead and one that has its costs. Do you really have any true friends? Or are they just in love with your reputation?

Or live in fear of it? You will never know.

How hard is hard? You may be able to handle yourself in a 'ruck' but will you be prepared when your reputation precedes you to have your legs blown away by a shotgun from a moving car when you are coming out of a restaurant with your wife? Think about it because this is what some 'hard' men have to contend with all their lives because of the path they have chosen to follow. Some are lucky and can escape that life, others not.

Do you think that last paragraph is over-dramatic? Then read the earlier books I mentioned and others like it to find out the truth.

Remember, reputations are sometimes used as a safety shield and other times they can be like a 'red rag to a bull'. People will see it as a challenge and come looking to test you.

At one stage Mike Tyson held the title as 'the baddest guy on the planet'. At one stage in his career he certainly looked it! His reputation alone had other heavy weight boxers wobbling at the knees! Some were beaten before ever stepping into the ring with Tyson, then suddenly Buster Douglas, an ordinary heavy weight, exploded the myth and the reputation by knocking Tyson out. Suddenly boxers were all coming out the woodwork, clamouring for a challenge where 6 months previously you wouldn't have seen them for dust! Amazing how things can change when the mighty fall! But did this all mean Tyson was a useless fighter? Of course not - he could/can still beat most of the best heavies out there and is still an awesome fighter in any arena - but it just goes to show you how the psychology of people can change and how their programming can be altered. Obviously Douglas and later Holyfield didn't bother to 'read the script' but went with their own beliefs.

When Rickson Gracie tastes defeat will it make any difference? Will people no longer wish to train with him and learn off him? I don't think so. Too much in this day and age has been placed on the 'baddest man' principle. Anybody can be king of the hill one day and bottom of the heap the next! For those of you out there striving for the 'hardman' tag, be sure you know what you are taking on.

Finally, as my good friend and fellow self protection instructor Jamie O'Keefe would say; *'Anybody can do anybody, they just have to find a way!'*

'Until you've lost your reputation, you never realise what a burden it was or what freedom really is'

Chapter 4

'Monsters do exist

'The belief in a supernatural source of evil is not necessary. Men alone are capable of every wickedness.' Joseph Conrad

We all have images of evil. In childhood evil was depicted in fairytales by wicked witches, goblins and giants. Although on the surface these stories seem no more than fantasy, many of them carried underlying messages. 'Little Red Riding Hood' for instance tells a child not to stop and talk with strangers. Hansel and Gretal informs us always leave a 'traceable' trail to your whereabouts so others can find you if you go missing and Goldilocks and the three bears lets us know not to wander into strange or unfamiliar places because you will not know what trouble or danger awaits you.

These stories and others gently ingrain the seed of awareness in a young child without frightening the life out of them.

I used to love as a youngster watching all those old horror films from Universal and Hammer. 'Dracula', 'Frankenstein,' The Wolfman', 'The Mummy' and many others.

I remember nagging my dad to sit up late and see these films.

I thought they were great and relished the chill they gave me.

It was a safe thrill because you were in the security of your own home. Deep down you knew these monsters didn't really exist.

This was all fine until after you had to go up the dark stairs to bed. I remember running up the stairs and swiftly into my room. Next a cautious inspection under the bed and inside the wardrobe and then a leap into bed to hide under the blanket.

After 5 minutes of sweating and using up vital oxygen I would surface, eyes first from out of the covers and survey the darkness of my room. My young and over active imagination used to run wild. The 'dressing gown hanging on the back of the door became a hideous ghost! My clothes draped on the chair in the corner became a shadowy figure. The wind blowing the curtain must be a vampire ready to pounce!

Its amazing what the mind can conjure up in times of fear. If you lose a grip on reality you can envisage all sorts of evil lurking in the darkened corners of your room.

When daylight arrived and I awoke, the room was as normal; all the things that had frightened me in the dark were now familiar objects with no sinister purposes. All was well until the next time!

The horror films of those years all depicted stories that had grown from myths and legends from every corner of the world. Every country had their tales of horror and ghosts. In the ages of no electricity for light and television, sitting down and telling 'ghost stories' was the common practise back then and from these stories spawned the creatures of the films.

In the innocence of childhood these creatures were make believe, but as I grew older and wiser I began to realise there were such things as monsters only they weren't vampires, werewolves or zombies, the worst monsters were humans, just like you and me!

The problem though, these monsters didn't hide in dark dungeons or haunted houses, they walk in among us as members of society, most unnoticed, unremarkable and indistinguishable from everybody else. They don't sprout fangs, they don't howl at the moon and they don't lurk in bushes, wearing a Halloween mask.

They mix with decent folk and hold good jobs. Some can be pillars of society. Local fundraisers and charity supporters. They may be well established with local councils or indeed the police.

If you read accounts of some of the world's worst serial killers, rapists or paedophiles, you will find most of them lead dual lives. Managing to keep their deprived dark side well hidden until they had to reveal it. Most were well educated, good looking, well spoken and charming plus clever and devious.

As the screen monsters would transform from normal beings into hideous monsters, metaphorically speaking so do the real monsters. When their craving for evil gets too strong then they show their true selves.

These people may not always be strangers to their victims. They can be work colleagues, friends, neighbours or shockingly, family members! When these people are caught by the police how many times have you heard friends or family say, 'I had no idea it was them, they seemed so normal.'

Remember a lot of these monsters are pure psychopaths. They have no conscience, so they can easily forget their horrific crimes and carry on their lives, putting their deeds away in a compartment in their minds.

Many may not commit another crime for months or years until some factor in their lives trigger them off again.

Several cases have documented wives living with their husbands and never even suspecting he was a serial rapist or killer.

Thankfully the manifestation of the serial killer is not as wide spread in the UK as the United States, but we have had our share. Neilson, Sutcliffe, West, Shipman. All living in society undetected for years before being discovered and in that time they took many innocent lives.

As mentioned previously one of America's worst serial killer, Ted Bundy, went undetected for many years and in that time murdered 35 plus victims. Bundy was a handsome and articulate college graduate who used his charm with the ladies as a weapon to eventually kill them. He was also extremely cunning Using both his knowledge of college campuses and his boyish good looks, he could walk around these sites with an armful of books and not look out of place. Also he used his devious mind to think up some ingenious ways of getting girls close to him. One was struggling around on crutches looking vulnerable. The other trying to strap something on top of his car with one of his arms in a false plaster cast. He knew his apparent helplessness would attract help and it normally did. After all how can an injured man be a threat to a girl?

Another Mass murderer in the US, John Wayne Gacy murdered 30 plus young men after hideously torturing them. He was a well-respected builder and a local fundraiser at the children's hospitals amongst other social duties.

He used his building business to pick up young guys new in town looking for work who then became his victims. Many ended up buried under his house and while this all went on he carried on a remarkably normal life! Some of his closest friends could not believe he was this monster, once he was brought to justice.

Somewhere though in each serial killers past is a pattern and many tell tale signs to what they can progress to! In Paul Britton's two excellent books 'The Jigsaw Man' and 'Picking up the Pieces', he explains this theory in great detail. Both books are well worth reading.

He believes like other criminal psychologists that the killer will always start his 'career' in a small way. Maybe torturing or killing small animals, then showing violence and abuse to people before working up to their ultimate goal, murder!

The serial killer or rapist is hardly ever spontaneous. They will travel areas for weeks or months in search of their ideal victim. They will show immense patience and restraint until the time is right. When they find their victim they will follow them for days or weeks, watching their routines, where they live, work etc. Then when the time is right they will strike. Most victims are not randomly picked; they have been picked for a reason. Of course some serial killers or rapists may select their victim on one viewing and commit their crime but even in that short space of time they will of thought it out and have a plan.

Most spontaneous murders are crimes of passion, not the work of a psychopath. Again if you study any of the famous cases, victims were carefully selected. If they fitted the 'model' in the mind of the killer that would do.

No murder is motiveless; no one is murdered for no reason. OK the reason may in some circumstances seem pointless to you or me, but not to the killer. Some victims may be murdered because they had the same colour hair or eyes as the killers 'mind model' and that will be sufficient cause to commit the crime. Sure it's not rational to us, but remember we are not dealing with a rational mind.

Remember the psychopath killer has no conscience or sense of guilt. Their crimes are based around power and control, everything else is secondary.

We can look at their heinous crimes and say that we can't believe that a human being can do these things to another. But if we look through history these things have been happening on a large or small scale for centuries.

Is it that we feel in the Millennium we should be more civilised? Maybe we should but these types of crimes just don't seem to go away. If you close your eyes at this moment and allow your mind to wander and conjure up the worst thing possible one human can do to another, I guarantee you it's been done for real, somewhere in this world. Man has a huge capacity for violence, killing and death. Could we not classify Hitler in the bracket of a psychopath and serial killer on a colossal scale?

I am not qualified to discuss the whys and wherefores that drive these people to execute these despicable acts. But I can educate others to realise these people are around us in society. Maybe sat next door to you on a bus or in a cafe.

Screen killers like Jason (Friday 13th), Michael Myers (Halloween) and of course Hannibal Lecter, have become cult figures and worshipped, basically on the strength of slaughtering innocent victims.

People view the serial killer as some entity that couldn't possibly come into their lives. They enjoy the chill of the screen version but still try and deny the real ones. Brushing the assumption aside by convincing themselves they are far and few between or those sort of things only happen to certain types of people. Wrong! When we accept monsters walk among us, we can start to make sure we don't fall victim to them!

'Beware of false prophets which come to you in sheep's clothing but inwardly they are ravaging wolves.'

Chapter 5
'Suffer little children'

The word paedophile has come to the forefront of our attention in recent years It seems a day doesn't go by when there is some reference to this sexual deviant in the newspapers or on the television. People have become more aware and more educated to this dangerously increasing threat to our children.

When I was young we all knew some 'strange man' or 'peculiar person' that hung around in the neighbourhood. Normally we would poke fun at them and run off. Some were probably harmless, others maybe not.

Although you were told by parents not to talk to strangers or accept sweets or lifts from them because they may harm you, you were never quite 100% sure exactly what harm they would do.

Many oddball characters hung around playing fields or playgrounds and although you were wary of them you didn't take that much notice. Looking back now you can see many potentially dangerous situations that thankfully didn't come to anything.

In this day and age though people's, awareness is much more perceptive, so to are the children's. They have to be because the paedophile rings seem to be growing like a disease.

Gone are the days when children can go off across playing fields or down to the local park on their own. A child's freedom seems to be snatched away from them by these evil predators. Most children's pleasures are now coming from playing computer games in the safety of their bedrooms. Young children can't even feel 100% safe in their front or back gardens!

The deeply harrowing cases in recent years of young kids being kidnapped, sexually abused and murdered leave a long and lasting impression on us all, especially if you are a parent of children yourself.

I find it hard personally to read accounts of these cases as it makes me feel deeply saddened and also avengingly angry at the same time. The days of kids enjoying innocent pleasures are gone, who do they trust anymore?

In days gone by authoritive figures in the community were the people to seek help from if your parents were not available. In some respects this still holds true, but there have been paedophile cases concerning clergy, teachers, sports coaches and youth club leaders. Homes where children went for shelter, care and safety have been exposed in some cases as the worst places for child abuse. This going undetected for years and years.

Or what about the child living in fear in their own homes suffering abuse at the hands of a family member over and over again. I just can't comprehend what drives people to do these things and what pleasure they derive from it. A child has a right to grow up into a mature adult. A child has a right to enjoy the pleasure of childhood and a child should have the trust of those they look up to most or love.

Paedophiles seem to be giving the authorities and police the run around. They ply their trade on the internet at every opportunity. They are housed next to schools, playgrounds or areas populated by young families and get away with it.

Known offenders, some profiled as 'probably will re-offend' are walking carelessly in society, trawling areas where kids are present day in day out without any problems.

When an innocent child is murdered, there is a massive out cry from all corners, but then nothing major is done. Parents have to grip hold of the first responsibility and educate their children on these matters because the problem does not look like it will go away and no authority seems to have a solution.

Following is an article I wrote some years back for 'Fighters' magazine for Martial Arts/Self Defence. The topic was safety and self defence for children. I felt it was fitting to include it in this chapter.

'Fighting chance for children'

Self defence techniques for children can be a controversial subject. Just what type of martial art moves should they be learning. If any at all? The old saying 'A little knowledge can be a dangerous thing!' springs to mind when kids and martial arts are mentioned. At the end of the day, when you analyse the subject, the majority of martial arts being taught to children have little or nothing to do with self protection at all. When some pervert preys on innocent children and decides to attack them, it won't matter if are Junior lightweight champion of Taekwondo or Judo. It won't matter how many Katas they know, how many medals or trophies they own or if they can twirl half a dozen anarchic martial art weapons, nine times out of ten they won't get away. Spending time practising the 100 metres dash maybe a better option!

Now I'm not against children learning martial arts, in fact I think it is a good thing. Let's face it a good three-quarters of martial art instructors income will come from the children's classes. but that aside children find at an early age discipline, respect, fitness, a good sense of belonging, competition and good fun in martial art classes. This is a good thing, they are the future of all martial arts in the UK and indeed the world. Also a child can gain great self confidence and if shy, the training can bring them out of them selves and help them in all walks of life and this training will stay with them to adulthood. But back to the subject of self defence. Many of the techniques taught to children may well discourage the school-yard bullies from messing with a certain child but this is very different from some adult attacker hell bent on doing a child harm.

I feel some parents may think that by their child practising a martial art that they will have a fighting chance against an assault if the unthinkable situation arrives. In some cases if the child is alert and the attacker careless, the child may be able to do something and run, but to be honest most of the techniques taught to kids, will not stand up in a real street attack.

These factors must be taken into consideration: a) Most children in martial arts practise against other children, where they may be able to throw another youngster or execute a perfect spinning hook kick to another kids head, against a large aggressive adult the technique will fail miserably . b) A real attack by an adult can be the most frightening and horrific experience they will ever encounter. What will a child be like when they are viciously attacked? c) There will be no referee, instructor, coach or teacher to call stop to the fight when it begins. It will be the child or the attacker!

These are just three of the important things to consider about effective techniques for children. Now on the other side of the coin some will say, children are not mentally mature enough to handle dangerous martial art techniques. They could use them against other children in a playground fight resulting in drastic consequences.

Or children should not be subjected to the truths about violence and the horrors of what is happening in today's society, they should be allowed to enjoy their time as kids and not grow up too fast.

Well, in the answer to all that I would say any parent that has lost a child through violent assault and see if they given the choice would have liked their child armed with some basic but effective techniques to at least have given them a fighting chance? I think they would say yes!

Today's society has deteriorated BADLY, surely our attitudes have to change towards children. Sometimes they can be more grown up than we give them credit for. I feel from when they are old enough to understand fully, 4 to 5 years old, you should tell them of the dangers they can face. Frighten them? Yes, to a degree, where they know it is serious and they listen. Teach them about safety and to make sure as parents, guardians, teachers, coaches, what ever, to do your utmost to maintain the standards. It's no use warning a child about the dangers out on the streets then the next day letting them go out to the shop on their own for some sweets because they are getting under your feet!

If you look into stories behind the tragedies of the deaths of young children a fair few were left to their own devices before the attack happened. Adults have a duty to protect children at all times even when you are screaming for a five-minute break. I am not talking off the top of my head as I have three children of my own aged 10, 12, and 15 years, and a complete handful. My wife and I over the years have found ourselves at breaking point on many occasions but we have never just sent the children out on the streets to get a minute's peace. I'm not saying it is easy, I'm no saint, it takes tremendous patience and willpower. How can you live with yourself if something happened to your child because you let them wander outside because you wanted to watch TV or chat to a friend!

Once you start instilling the warnings in your child about talking to strangers, accepting lifts, whatever, then make sure they understand always the first line of self defence, prevention.

Self defence techniques from an instructor's point of view I feel must be done as a separate issue away from normal martial art classes. First you must make the children understand that this is something different and that the techniques are for defence against a serious assault by a larger and older person and to be used only for when they feel their life in danger. (Not an easy task but it can be done). It is a good thing to let the parents know what the classes will entail so they can choose whether they want their child exposed to this side of martial art.

Next prime the children with stories and facts of what has happened to other children (not graphically) and explain how they could have avoided what had happened.

When you feel they understand, then you can begin simple, easy to learn self defence moves. Nothing fancy or complex, these things simply will not work. Exclude the majority of throwing and locking techniques, they will not stand up under the test of real fighting. An instructor has got to work with techniques that are practical for the child not what he can make work.

The system I teach called Kempo Goshin Jitsu has a vast array of techniques, strikes, throws, locks, chokes, pressure points, etc, but only about 10% of the technique will be given to a child for self protection classes. They must know how to attack the vital points on an adult. Points that can be hit quickly and effectively, not having to rely on strength. These are eyes, nose throat, groin, knees, shins.

Remember a kid is closer to low targets and their centre of gravity is lower. Kicking into the knee/shin or stomping an instep will break a hold for an escape. Punching, palm heel or hammering the groin will also get a release, small children are on the right level for a good groin kick.

If picked up, head butting the nose with front or rear of the head is a surprise and effective move. Punching or palm heeling the nose also works. Striking the eyes with thumbs or a spread claw hand is also effective. Punching , chopping, elbowing or hammering the throat from the front or rear can break any strong hold if you can get to it!

Teaching combinations of knee/shin kicks with strikes to the groin and then into the eyes and throat can devastate even an adult attacker and buy time to escape.

In my system I don't expect a child to throw a large adult over their head or destroy them into unconsciousness with a barrage of blows. But .-some well placed strikes against an overconfident and unaware adult can help them escape a bad situation and keep their lives, which ultimately is the only importance.

At close range kids can bite and gain instant release. If lifted in frontal body holds, biting into the earlobe, nose or neck will make the opponent drop you. Follow up with a kick to the shin or groin after the bite and you are away, safe.

If they are grabbed from the rear with a hand over their mouths, teach them to manoeuvre the attackers little finger into their mouths and bite down hard or sink their teeth anywhere onto the hand or wrist.

We all know the risk of biting but if you are fighting for your life what choice have you got? Furthermore a bite mark can be identified later if the attacker is caught by the law.

Bending little finger joints is also an effective technique for children, not a lot of strength required, but breaking and twisting the little finger joints can take the biggest assailants down.

Also teaching makeshift weaponry out of things a child may carry with them, is also an essential part of their protection programme. Books, comics, pencils, toys, coins, schools bags, etc, can be taught to excellent effect with a little time and imagination. Striking the above targets already mentioned with these makeshift weapons can magnify the blow a hundred fold and make them that much more effective.

These suggestions are no means complete they are just some ideas for instructors and parents to think about. Some of the things said may be controversial, but I whole heartily believe if children don't learn effective self defence moves from an early age of 8 years then many more tragedies will occur?

Society has in recent times thrown up sick individuals and a parent cannot always be there in life to protect their children surely its worth taking the risk to let children learn in the proper way the more brutal and practical techniques to give them a Fighting Chance?

Remember prevention is better than cure. We don't want our children faced with a scenario where they are fighting for their lives. (who does!). Let's not let them get to that stage, let's look to avoid all together and if help them to develop enough perception to know when a dangerous situation is developing. They need to trust their instincts when something doesn't feel quite right.

There are times as parents where you will obviously have to put your child in the momentary care of another adult, but you must first feel satisfied they are safe.

I am amazed the amount of parents that will bring a child to my Martial Arts class for the first time and leave them there without viewing the class or watching me as a coach.

I try to encourage parents and children to watch a class first or for the parent to view their child train, so that they know exactly what the class entails. You have to be so careful these days teaching kids. Although I must say there are stricter and better screening methods for coaches now than there used to be.

For many years swimming instructors and pool side assistants jobs had been known to be seeked by paedophiles.

Parents, do check out coaches, instructors, youth leaders, nannies, child minders, babysitters etc, satisfy yourself that your child is in good hands, don't take things on face value.

In recent times kids having a 'sleep over' at a school friends house has become popular. I am wary of this and make sure my kids, my wife and myself know not only the child but their parents and the set up regarding their home life. Paranoid? No, just cautious, I don't fancy the idea for my child sleeping in a strange environment. They would really have to be good and trustworthy friends before I would allow this. Think about that issue? In this day and age you unfortunately just cannot be that sure, can you?

Also the American trend of 'trick and treating' at Halloween can present a danger for children, if they do this alone or without an adult present. Knocking on complete stranger's doors in the dark of an October evening isn't the safest of pursuits. On the surface the trend is harmless fun for children but below the surface you can see hidden dangers. By all means let you child go 'trick or treating' but accompany them!

Every child obviously has to eventually leave 'the nest' you have just got to make sure they are prepared when they go.

As a parent you will do well to keep up with the latest trends and happenings in your childs world. Times change. They are not the same as your childhood.

Sexual predators also change. They unfortunately move with the trends too. They make it their business to do so.

No longer are they offering sweets or the chance to see some 'puppies' to intice a child. Now they are offering Pokemon cards, wrestling figures, computer games. Or for the older child, mobile phones, chart C.D's or drugs. They are cunning and devious, again on outwards appearances quite normal. They are not all 'dirty old men in raincoats!'

Some work in pairs not alone, which makes it all the more difficult for a child to fight back. They have been known to use substances like chloroform to drug and subdue a struggling or screaming child.

I read recently in a national newspaper that a woman paedophile has been trying to snatch children by posing as a social worker. She was going to selected homes and trying to take a child from their family. Luckily she didn't succeed. But it proves the lengths these people will go to, to fulfil their evil needs. Don't make it easy for these people by allowing young children to go on errands on their own or walk a few blocks to a friends house. There shouldn't be a time where you don't know where your child is. The very young must not be let out of your sight. Too many children have been snatched because of these things. It doesn't matter how close they are to home it still can happen. It's like locking your front door when you go to work for the day but not locking it when you 'pop' around the corner to your local newsagent. These people can be opportunists and seize any chance to take a lone child.

For older children a mobile phone has become the latest fashion accessory and a must have thing! But the phone can be much more than an expensive toy. Impress upon your child to use it wisely. Allow call time to contact a parent if you have a delay or change of plan when you are out. Also use it to let people know when you have arrived safely at your destination when you plan to come home. It only takes a minute but puts everybody at ease and they know help can only be a call away. The mobile is a great modern tool of self protection if used wisely.

When you drop a child off at a party, event etc let the organiser know who will be picking them up later and also leave a contact number for them. Make sure you do the same thing at schools, clubs etc. The paedophile predator who is desperate enough may pretend to be a family member or friend to get to a child. Cut off all their avenues to get at their target. Make it as difficult as you can.

Yes it's unfortunate we have to do these things, but a little time spent on proactive precautions can save a life time of tragedy and regret.

Lastly I mentioned earlier that authorities are not doing much proactively to stem the evil of child abuse. But I have immense respect for the NSPCC and Child line who work tirelessly to help abused children. It is a great pity children have got to get to this stage of abuse before it is discovered.

'When the fox hears a rabbit scream, he comes running, but not to help!'

Chapter 6
Understanding aggression
'Aggression is a product of modern society'

The society we live in today is one of aggressive actions and behaviour. Everywhere you go you will experience examples of this. Aggressive sales aggressive bosses, aggressive drivers, aggressive shoppers and so one and so on.

The modern environment is built on aggression, this is alright if it is channelled correctly but most of it becomes misplaced and people cannot 'switch off' this side of their nature and let it overspill into other areas of their life. For example, the company boss who is used to control and power in his job environment who believes when he is behind the wheel of his car he has to demand the same respect from other road users and when he doesn't, resorts to road rage tactics. I have seen this happen first hand and believe me it is true and is happening all the time.

Fights, violence and abuse break out over the most trivial of things on a daily basis. I have seen work colleagues come to blows over a 'silly' job related matter that later in the 'cold light of day' seems totally absurd. The pressure that society can put on you will sometimes reach 'boiling point' and then somebody somewhere is going to 'get it'.

You don't have to be doing anything remotely wrong to suddenly find yourself in some sort of confrontational situation with some person who is hell bent on making you the target of their aggression.

You can be sat in your car at the traffic lights and quite casually glance at the car next to you and catch the driver's eye and find them glaring with a hard stare because you dared look in their direction. Some people have been battered for this, how incredible. But if you are not aware of the signs you will become a victim.

I have walked down a street and 200 yards up the road a youth is walking on the same side as me and as he gets closer suddenly the chest puffs up, arms splay and he gets the arrogant spring to his stride and begins some mean eye contact. Why?

Am I so frightening? am I such a threat to him, or have I just dared to walk in the same space as him?

It's crazy, these days I laugh to myself and ignore it. Obviously this person must be so insecure of themselves they have to put on this 'strutting peacock act'. Years ago I would have taken up the eye contact challenge because in my younger days I was probably as insecure in my abilities as them! But with age comes wisdom and through adversity truth, I no longer feel I have anything to prove, but if you didn't feel this way can you see how you would be in a confrontational situation every day of the week? Most of them borne out of nothing. People have been known to verbally abuse and physically attack others for being in a 10 items only check out in a supermarket with 12 items in their baskets! Big deal! But for some with their misguided sense of aggression this seems an ideal situation to get rid of it and they will think nothing of doing so.

How many blokes have you met that will quite joyously relate to you on a Monday morning at work the good 'kick in' they gave to someone on a Saturday night for life threatening reasons such as 'spilling my pint', stood in my spot at the bar, 'Looking at my girl', or supporting the 'wrong' football team. They are proud of it and can't see how pointless it all is. These guys will think nothing of giving somebody a good hiding and then going for a drink to celebrate.

Violence will happen anywhere, anytime, day or night, people have got to understand and be prepared.

A few years ago I taught a group of ladies Self Protection. A few weeks into the course one of the ladies came to me and said she had been attacked the previous evening. I asked her what had happened. She told me she had drove into a car park space at a large multi complex cinema and was just taking her keys from the ignition when a man appeared by her drivers' side door. It was a summer's evening and her window was down. He began to rant and rave about her stealing his parking space and then without any warning punched her in the face and strode off!

She was in shock and pain, but she told me the biggest surprise was that he had unreservedly hit her. This is a prime example of the random and mindless violence that just happens. I explain more about this in my book 'In Your Face.'

Today's perpetrators of mindless' violence have no code or ethics, they will mug, abuse and hurt man, women and child, any age, colour or creed.

I recently read the excellent autobiography of the late and great Lenny Mc Lean entitled 'The Guv'nor'. He was a prolific bare knuckle boxer who had also in his time cruised on the wrong side of the law and had used violence many times when necessary. But he even said in the book that today's criminals are 'little shits', who have no moral values or codes, they will think nothing of battering an old age pensioner for £10.00 in their handbag. They are a different breed to criminals of yesteryear, who only dealt with their own kind. This is true, each day the newspapers are full of these random and brutal assaults on people for no apparent reason.

Being involved in the Self Protection scene for many years not much surprises me now in the lengths certain people will go to to court violence.

It still sickens me but does not surprise me. I realise what these people are capable of and how they operate and it is down to myself and fellow instructors alike to educate the general public on these matters when they seek our assistance.

The most important thing is to get people out of the 'it won't happen to met mind set, because it can and will, no one is immune and it doesn't matter who you are or what your fighting skills may be it still doesn't guarantee a thing. Awareness, evaluation and avoidance are the keys, violence is the last resort but if you use it, be brutal and be clinical and then get away.

When all the talking is done it is no good trying to appeal to the street thugs better nature, they haven't got one! Then it will be physical and those who condemn pre-emptive striking, head butts, biting, gouging and all the other unpleasantries of close quarter fighting will wish they had practised them because they will be needed when the 'chips are down'.

What reasons can be given for these types of motiveless attacks? Why does it happen for no apparent reason? In his book

'Bar-room Brawling' American Self Defence teacher and ex-doorman Peyton Quinn comments that for years he couldn't understand why he was the subject of said mindless attacks in bars and clubs until he came up with the answer that he was enjoying himself too much in these surroundings, having too much fun.

These people that executed the violence could not stand this as they were experiencing so much pain in their own miserable lives so they had to give him some of that pain to make him understand.

This is a great theory, this is the misplaced aggression we spoke of earlier on and one we should take time to understand.

You see these people who offer misplaced aggression hate you to be happier than them or have a better car, clothes, watch, shoes, girlfriend, whatever, it doesn't matter as long as they feel justified in battering you for it!

These said persons are the unexploded walking time bombs looking for any excuse to trigger them off into a frenzy of violence. Beware of them because they are everywhere in society.

When I worked in a timber yard for many years that served the public I met these people on a regular basis. If you couldn't provide the goods they wanted or took too long they would explode like you wouldn't believe, going from raged disbelief to verbal abuse and then offering you physical violence. I met some weird and wonderful characters in that period of time and learned a hell of a lot about human psychology. I had 15 years of dealing with these type of people 'although there was the good as well'! I must admit I became a 'little crazy' at the time too! But now I can see how totally pointless it was.

Self Defence manuals will tell you how to avoid the mugger or rapists. They will instruct you in safety and avoidance techniques, i.e. don't walk in dangerous neighbourhoods; accept lifts from strangers, etc, which is all good and sound advise. But none prepare you or even discuss in any detail about misplaced aggression and the type of persons who execute it. You must become aware of it because you can follow all the self defence codes to the letter but still fall foul to this type of predator! Beware and be safe!

Chapter 7
Channelling your own aggression correctly

'If you are not in control of yourself you cannot possibly control anyone else'

In the last chapter we explored the tell tale signs of aggression in other people, but can you recognise it in yourself?

As I mentioned at the start of this book, I had to do some self analysis to come to the conclusions I write about in this text. One of the things I had to acknowledge was at certain stages in my life I was overly aggressive and was easy to anger.

Looking back at one such stage of my life, I can see stress was building and I didn't know how to react to it at the time. I was under a lot of pressure in a job I no longer enjoyed but because of my position I was still answerable to people. I had also a young family at home and was experiencing many sleepless nights. This along with my heavy training regime for the Martial Arts I was on my way to burn out! The first inkling I really had was when I visited a new health centre and they were giving free health checks to new patients. Being a fanatical fittest 'freak' you can imagine my surprise when they diagnosed I had high blood pressure. I was shocked to say the least! I didn't smoke, drank alcohol moderately and followed a healthy eating plan, why did I have high blood pressure?

Of course after examing my lifestyle I know it was stress but it took me some time to find my answers. Because of my lifestyle I was becoming more aggressive and at times said and did things I now regret. I would 'blow up' when I didn't agree with something or things weren't going right, particularly at work. I was confrontational with co-workers, customers and management alike. Basically I had a go at anybody. I was like a bull terrier and probably about as intimidating.

Not all the situations at that stage of my life were of my own making, I did encounter in my job (timberyard/sawmill foreman on the docks), some pretty obnoxious, rude and plain nasty people. The trouble was I was at a point in time where I was fighting fire with fire. Very little compromise or tact!

I laugh now at some of the situations I got myself in but to be honest I suspect quite a few people didn't like me or thought I was a 'little crazy'. But through all that, deep down I was/am a good person I just lost my way slightly.

I was training hard in very physical contact Martial Arts and the aggression wasn't being channelled correctly. In training I hurt a lot of people who didn't really deserve that treatment, but I saw no wrong or didn't realise it. I truly believe the environment or the circles we choose to live in effect how we feel and our outlook on life.

When I was made redundant from my job it gave me the final push to pursue my life long ambition to be a full-time professional Martial Arts instructor. I also qualified myself as a fitness coach and received diplomas in sports coaching and psychology.

It opened new doors and breathed fresh air into my life. With this new direction I also accomplished another ambition to write books. Don't get me wrong I am not some self made millionaire, rolling in money but I have got a worthwhile life, where I am my own boss and I control my own destiny. I still work hard, putting many hours in the gym, training hall and behind my desk but what I'm getting that I didn't get before is job satisfaction. I can see an end product to my efforts and work. I feel I am making a worth while contribution and that is just as good as making millions. As soon as I left the old job my stress was gone, blood pressure fine and the aggression I began to channel.

I was in a different environment, with different people. Not negative or aggressive, this changed me greatly. Don't misunderstand me I still have to work on controlling my anger, aggression but I feel I am a totally different person to five years ago. I have achieved a better balance in my life and I get rid of my aggression in a controlled manner in the training halls and it very rarely overlaps into my social or private life. My family also give me the strength and love to keep me changing and progressing in the right direction.

Please don't think I'm a saint, I am not but inwardly I am a better person than 5 or 6 years ago. Because I have nothing to prove. I

have tested myself in many pressurized areas and survived, I am not now driven
with the same conviction to test myself to those extremes anymore.

But what has my little self confession to do with you, you might be asking? Well I managed to identify my 'weaknesses', can you identify yours or even more do you feel you have any in the first place?

Aggression is a strange thing, sometimes like myself I didn't even realise it was a problem. But now I can see it can be. People will view you in a different light and will not be so forth coming if they sense you are hostile. It's just like reaching out to pat a dog that suddenly starts growling at you, you will quickly retract your hand and step back. I don't want people to treat me like that. I don't want to be the bully that I used to fear!

Being assertive is being different to aggressive. It's the same as asking somebody do you know the difference between asking another person 'What's the matter?' and 'What's your problem?'. You will certainly get two different reactions to which one you ask! Confidence, assertiveness and being self-assured can be admirable qualities but don't let them become cockiness, aggression and brashness.

If you harbour any 'hot spots', you better start learning to lose them because they will only control you and in the end be your down fall.

What do I mean by 'hot spots?' Well are you a 'road rager?' Do you fly off the handle.' at the most trivial of things? I did, until I learnt that to control a situation or indeed another person you first have to have self control.

Things aren't always black and white or as you first presume. We are all too ready to make snap judgements or opinions without always knowing the full story.

I will relate a tale to you that will illustrate what I mean. During the bad spell of weather we had after last Christmas, I was walking back home after work really soaked to the skin from yet another shower of rain! I debated whether to take a short route straight home or take a slight detour and buy the morning's newspaper.

I decided to get the newspaper and carried on walking. As I neared the newsagents I noticed the shutters pulled down. The shop was obviously shut. I was just about to start cursing under my breath about how useless the newsagent was, when I saw a small handwritten notice on the door, that read 'Sorry we are closed. Family bereavement. Our father died last night'. It stopped me in my tracks and I mentally apologised for being so hasty. I was ready to 'go off on one' without knowing the facts.

It's like the story of the irate driver behind a car travelling extremely slowly. This driver cursed, swore, blasted the horn and shook his fist all the way along a stretch of road because this other driver was making him late for work. Eventually the car came to an abrupt halt in the middle of the road and the seething driver of the car behind got out and ran to the driver's side of the stopped car and banged on the window, shouting, 'What's the f-----problem with you pal?' When be looked into the car, the driver was slumped over the wheel and it transpired afterwards that he had suffered a fatal heart attack. The irrate driver was mortified and walked away suitably subdued.

You see life has a way of 'throwing up' unusual circumstances and we should all use the gift of fore sight before the event and not hind sight after it!

Learning to rid yourself of 'hot spots' is a learning experience. Years ago if I was walking along the road and somebody shouted out 'Oiw, you bald w ---- r I would have reacted extremely aggressively. But these days I wouldn't even register it. After all why should I, I know I'm not one ..... well bald maybe. But what I'm trying to get over is the streetwise aggressor or trouble maker will use these strategies to 'test the water' and see if you are a prime candidate for a 'wind up'. Don't give them the pleasure. Infact go the other way. If you are called a bald w ---- r, say 'How the hell did you know?' It's not the response they're expecting.

I come from an Irish background, the surname may have given you a clue! My parents are Irish and the majority of my relatives, although I was born in the UK. When the spate of 'Irish jokes' were the in thing, I laughed along and told a few myself but I found if the tables were turned with an 'English' joke it didn't go down to well. Here is an absolute gem that always guaranteed me a dumb struck audience or had me running for the door, or in those days daring somebody to make something of it. It illustrates the subject perfectly about not rising to the bait and retaliating with a very clever remark. Beware though this one could start a fight! But hey, shouldn't everybody take what they dish out?

Joke:- An Irishman was sitting at the bar in a pub enjoying a nice pint of beer and reading the newspaper. Just then two English fellows walked in and one says to the other, *'Hey look, there's Paddy over there, I'm going to wind him up,' 'Bet you can't replies his mate?' 'OK a tenner says I can',* retorts the other guy.

So off he goes to the bar and says to the Irishman. *'Hey Paddy did you know St. Patrick was an Englishman?'* The Irishman fellow keeps on reading his paper. *'Paddy, I said St. Patrick was an Englishman'* Still no response. The guy goes back to his mate, dejected. *'No luck',* he tells him. *'What did you say to him?'* asks the other fellow. *'Well I told him St. Patrick was an Englishman'. 'I'll get him going and claim that tenner',* replies his friend and walks off to the bar.

'Hey Paddy, did you know that St Patrick was a c--t?' he tells the Irishmen. Still not a flicker of emotion comes to the Irish fellow's face. The Englishman pulls the newspaper down from the Irishman hands and says *'Hey, did you hear what I said, 'St, Patrick was a c--t!'* The Irishman coolly takes a sip of his beer and tells the Englishman. 'I know, your mate told me already!!'...Every one laughing?

Joke apart, the lesson is to keep your cool and use your brains to sort out the situation rather than to resort to verbal and physical violence. It takes greater skill to handle a situation with cool dialogue than it does to go into a rage and start swinging punches. If the circumstances require a physical response then let it be ICE'Y aggression rather than 'fiery' aggression.

Allowing the 'red mist' to form over your eyes and to become completely out of control, is a one-way ticket to defeat and ultimately self-destruction. Learn to use your head for thinking) and you can avoid most trouble but also develop a more powerful weapon than your anger or your fists. Some people will inhabit places where trouble is always on the menu and find themselves ending up in volatile confrontations on a regular basis and not really knowing how to deal with them. Firstly, why go to these places at all? It's like saying 'Every time I put my hand in the oven I get burnt!' The solution to that problem is don't put your hand in there! So don't go to establishments or areas where you will encounter trouble. If you can avoid it, then you can avoid feeling intimidated or threatened, which in turn means you don't have to use the aggressive side of your nature.

Obviously you can end up in situations not of your own making, just being in the wrong place at the wrong time and you will have to think on your feet.

The following scenarios I am going to illustrate are ways of using cunning, guile, humour or bull shit to get yourself out of a 'sticky' confrontation without it deteriorating into violence. Some of the methods can be offensive and extreme, it would serve you well to let the people with you know you may use these schemes if trouble is brewing

Scenario Example 1

You are having a quiet drink at the bar when you notice across the way somebody 'eye-balling' you menacingly. This can be an extremely uncomfortable situation for some people. For the aggressive person it's a red rag to a bull! If you are looking for trouble just return their gaze and shout 'Have you got a f ----- g problem with me pal?' Now watch the sparks fly! Remember we are trying to control an emotional outburst and explore other ways of dealing with the problem.

One way is to ignore it. Register the look and store it in your mind but on the surface ignore it. If you catch the stare initially hold eye contact fleetingly, then coolly break contact without showing any emotion. Don't glance away quickly as this looks like a sign of fear or weakness and this will probably spur the 'looker' on. If you don't have to stay in the pub for any particular reason drink up and leave for another venue. Make sure your 'friend' doesn't follow. Fighting over your presence in a pub just isn't worth the hassle. If you're leaving gives the 'watcher' a sense of victory so be it. They must be of a pretty shallow nature to get a kick from this! Hopefully you're intelligent enough to walk away and see beyond it.

Scenario Example 2

Same situation, what if the person comes closer and continues their staring? You now in a friendly manner can say 'Excuse me mate, do I know you? The reason I ask is that you keep staring at me? Now let's see where this could get worse.

They reply 'I'm looking at you because I think you're a w--k-r!' Keep it cool and smile. Now in a low and controlled voice say. 'Look the last thing I need is trouble tonight, Ive just last week got out of prison after 2 years for an assault charge, I'm still on probation and I ain't going back in for you. So let me just enjoy my beer, what do you say?' See if the ploy works. Remember it's got to be practised to be believable unless this guy is really got it in for you, he just might figure he's taking on the wrong person. It's got to be worth a try.

You can work variations on this play. If you look the part you can tell the 'would be troublemaker' that you have just done a 5 year stint in the paras and you've seen enough action to last you a life time. Or inform them you are an off duty policeman and you just want a quiet drink. If you don't want it to get aggressive practise having a few lines 'up your sleeve', it has got to be better than rolling around on the floor! Even if you think you could win the fight!

Scenario Example 3
You are having a quiet drink/meal with your lady and a loud abusive drunk approaches your table. He says 'Hey pal, that's one ugly bitch you're sat with!' What do you do? This is a family restaurant, it's quiet, respectable, do you really want to kick off in here?

What's the usual response? For the average man, it's to stand up abruptly and say something like, 'How dare you, that's my wife you're speaking about'. Righteous indignation won't cut any ice here. This person isn't going to apologise and walk away. You see, this is his 'starter for ten'; he is testing the water to see your reaction. So give him something he doesn't expect and diffuse the situation. Get up and walk a distance from the table and at the same time gesture to him and say 'Can I have a word?' If he wants to save face he will have to follow. When he comes keep an arms length distance and say 'look, the last thing I need is any hassle. My wife there has been diagnosed recently to have terminal cancer. She only has months to live; I'm trying to give her a special night out. I'd appreciate it if you left us alone?'

Watch the look register on their face. If you pull it off right it's a gem. If not at least you gave this person a chance to walk.

Again think of variations on this theme there are many if you think about it. Extreme? Yes. But if it avoids a fight, exceptable.

If you honestly believe this person is a threat and you have to take physical attack (remember this is your last option), use icy aggression.

When that person snarls. 'I said that's one ugly bitch you got with you'.

Coolly look at her and then glance at the 'aggressor' and say 'You know what you're right she is f ----- g ugly! (or alternatively), 'Yes she is ugly but only compared to other women' While his befudled brain is sorting this remark out, use it as a trigger to hit him with a hard pre emptive shot and leave!

Scenario Example 4

This is the other way around and a troublemaker insults you by informing your lady what he thinks of you. If she is a 'player' of the game she can have a ready response, like this example.

'Owe love, what are you doing with an ugly tosser like him, you must be desperate?' Reply. 'I'm with him because he is loaded and hung like a donkey!' Quite a conversation stopper!!

Out-witting or de-escalating people is a definite skill. You should practise remarks and conversation on a regular basis For a martial artist you should hone dialogue as much as your best punch or kick otherwise you will always go for the physical response.

I have had friends who were not 'fighters' but were absolute masters of dialogue, one liners and wit. They diffused many situations by using these skills and it was a talent I tried to inherit. A good mate of mine, Scott, talked himself out of many a 'hiding' with his brillant dialogue skills. My mentor in these skills though was an old work buddy Eddie Lane, sadly he passed away a few years ago. When I worked with him he was in his early 60's and he was a master of the one line put down and smart retort. He used to have me crying with laughter with his dry humour and wit. He was totally dead pan when he delivered his lines and people couldn't figure if he was serious or not. We worked together in a busy timber yard and some of the customers, were to say the lest rude and aggressive, but Eddie never raised to the bait. He would just use his wit and sarcasm m. This was just a few of his specials. Customer 'Anybody f--k--g serving in this place?' Ed - 'Yes, I'll just get my tennis racket' Customer - 'Drinking tea again?' Ed - 'No this ones coffee actualy' Customer - 'This timber,s full of f--k--g knots!'

Ed - 'Yes, they just don't make trees without branches'
Aggression can be replaced with humour or sarcasm (read 'No one fears when Angry' by Jamie O'Keefe). But sometimes be prepared for the recipient not to share your sense of fun!

Human nature can be strange sometimes. We can be more hurt by an insult, put down or smart remark than we are with actually being physically struck.

If you get easily offended you must start to erase those 'hot spots' now. Don't react to being insulted with fiery aggression this is exactly the response your would be tormentor is looking for. They are priming you for a sucker punch as soon as you respond. Ignore it or learn to be more subtle about the way you handle the situation.

Everybody has a certain part of their body or characteristic they are not happy with and they are aware of and some people will exploit this fact given the chance. Example list -Big ears, big nose, bald, spotty, fat, skinny, scruffy, nervous twitch, stutter, hard of hearing, short sighted, slow speech, nervous, picks nose, etc etc, Add to this racial comments or religious ones, you can see if you are sensitive to one or more of these you are going to feel pretty uptight some days.

Remember the old saying, 'Sticks and stones will break my bones but names will never hurt me!' This holds true, don't allow words to wound you. Sure they can upset you but don't let them offend or control you. If you don't know the person that is calling you these names, it can't be personal, so let it run like water off a duck's back.

You may encounter aggressive people in your job calling you names or hurling abuse but if they don't know you it's not personal. We will look at how to handle this in a later chapter. For now learn not to fly off the handle.

I have taken aggression therapy classes where the participants will face up to each other and shout, curse and insult each other in turn. The idea for the recipient of the abuse is to stay calm and think 'under fire' and try to calm and deescalate the situation. No stone is unturned with the insults, the more personal the better. In the end you don't even listen to them, you know it is just the modern day street thugs entry technique to gauge your reaction. Years ago if I was called a 'little bald bastard' I probably would have reacted like a lunatic, now it's not going to phase me. I have done so many aggression therapy classes it's just 'play'. It positively cannot hurt me anymore. I can try to de-escalate and diffuse or I can come back with a witty retort, but I won't come back with a physical response unless I feel my well being is threatened. I have extended my 'cut out' point and built better tolerance and this is definitely the way to go.

If you don't try and control aggression in the long run it will affect personal relationships, working relations and gradually drag you down. You will not have many true friends and it will bring you a lot of heartache and trouble. When you are a young man you might think who gives a damn but as you get older you will see a different side. You may then want to change the way you are but what damage have you done before this decision?

While I'm writing this book the nation is yet again in the grip of a TV soap drama. This time it is 'Eastenders' and the 'Who shot Phil Mitchell' puzzle.

Steve McFadden who plays Phil, done a superb job of getting you to hate him. His bullying, aggression, insults and violence made him everybody's enemy and it was only a matter of time before he got his 'come uppance.'

Of course this is only the fantasy world of soaps, or is it? This can be an accurate portrayal of an individuals lifestyle. There are many real accounts of the above scenario happening. You see when you use aggression, bullying and violence as tools of the trade you have to always live with the fact you may encounter bigger and worse violence back. Beware, get a grip on your aggression, channel it correctly. Keep it on a leash, only to be released in time of emergency and then use it with icy cool precision not as a 'red mist'.

This chapter is a vital one for people looking to understand and control aggression in others. Firstly you must start with yourself. *'Whoever fights monsters should see to it that in the process he does not become a monster. For when you look long into an abyss, the abyss looks into you'* Robert Ressler Ex. Chief of the FBI behavioural science dept.

Chapter 8
'The Ticking Timebomb'

'I was just in the wrong place, at the wrong time'

Earlier we mentioned the 'Ticking Timebomb', called misplaced aggression. This is one of the prime reasons for people to suddenly 'Fly off the handle' or 'Lose it'. In todays society this type of aggression is responsible for a huge majority of so called 'mindless attacks'.

Society has created high degrees of pressure in one shape or form. In the workplace the employee has been pushed and pushed to gain better results, better work ethic, more production and so on and so on.

Staff shortages has put more work load and burden onto other individuals and so builds the stress to boiling point.

Do you remember the Michael Douglas film 'Falling down' about a mild mannered office worker who suddenly decided not to take any more 'crap' from society and went on the 'Rampage'. This is a reasonably true portrayal about how people feel when the pressure gets too much.

Some people have just 'upped' and disappeared completely after telling their partner that they are just nipping out for a moment. There are hundreds of cases of missing people who just decided to go off and leave everything behind. Was the pressure too much?

Others commit suicide because they can't face up to their pressures and choose this method as an escape route.

Then we have the person who because of maybe pressure in the workplace, at home, or with a relationship takes it out in the form of violence. The 'letting off of steam' becomes a physical gesture.

Instead of facing up to the real problem in their lives they decide to get some retribution by picking on an innocent party and venting their anger and frustration out on them.

These so called 'mindless acts of violence' are far from mindless. As I mentioned earlier no act of violence is mindless, there is always a motive.

The victim can be badly beaten or murdered, make no mistake, misplaced aggression can be a killer. Just look at the recent 'road rage' incident involving the criminal Kenneth Noye. This ending in the fatal stabbing of Stephen Cameron. He tragically confronted the wrong man and paid the price. This is why you must be aware of this type of aggression whenever you decide to confront somebody. People have been battered for simply asking if a person could stop parking outside their house or to stop their dog 'messing' on their front lawn.

Victims have commented after a confrontation that they had only accidently bumped into a person and spilt their drink or unknowingly drove into another person's parking space. Yes people have been kicked senseless for these seemingly innocuous 'crimes'.

Old age pensioners have been intimidated, pushed around and beaten because they had the audacity to suggest to some youths that they moderate their language or pick up their regarded litter. The older generation who fought and lived through war times expect some respect and most believe they should have it. But it doesn't work like that now. The society we live in has very little respect for anybody, not least the elderly.

When I was young and an elderly person may have caught you doing something wrong and gave you a stern 'telling off', you listened and were then on your way. In these days they will most lightly receive a mouthful of abuse for their trouble and probably a broken nose! Times have certainly changed.

But why? Today nobody wants to be told what to do, nobody wants to be proved wrong. Everybody is determined to be number one, the best, they see it as an insult to be corrected, pulled up or reprimanded. There unfortunately isn't a lot of respect in society. There are some smashing kids, teenagers and young people but also there are plenty of 'little shits', that have no regard for people or property. They all want to be would be 'gangsters' and tough guys. The drug culture and over excess of alcohol can lead to the problems. This makes people unreasonable, unpredictable and irrational. Some would sell their own grandmother for a line of cocaine. They will not be reasoned with. Their misplaced aggression will be vented on you if you get in their way or dare question their actions.

You may be in the wrong place at the wrong time and become the victim of their aggression and violence. Look at the recent case of the poor lady that was badly beaten and raped along a canal towpath by a gang of youths. Don't think for one minute gender or age will save you. Sometimes the world can be a despicable place!

The road rage driver is a classic example of misplaced aggression. He may be late for an appointment, just had an argument with his partner etc, etc, and when you drive too slowly in front of him he will snap, venting all this frustration onto you. He targets you to relieve the stress he is feeling. Some totally normal people will turn into monsters behind the wheel of a car. It's what I call the 'Jeckal and Hyde' syndrome.

A mild mannered individual suddenly goes through a metamorphsis to become this creature of hate and anger. Blasting his horn, cursing, swearing, gesturing and generally losing any self control.

If you encounter such a person do not under any circumstances get out of your car or confront them, keep on driving and hopefully you will never see them again. Remember it is not personal, you just happen to be there at the time. Don't make it worse. If you can't immediately drive away, then make sure your windows and doors are secure. Talk through a small crack in your side window if required to but don't wind the windows down or attempt to get out.

Being confronted by a road rager can be a frightening experience. Expect if they can't get to you, for them to kick, punch or hit your vehicle in frustration. Again don't let that faze you. Drive off as soon as the opportunity arrives.

I have been in a few situations when somebody has confronted me with all the signs of 'road rage'. If I had wanted to, I could have physically dealt with the problem without raising too much of a sweat, but I choose to drive on and not get involved. What's the point of all that hassle, why let some idiot spoil your day? I leave them because the way I figure it, their lives must be 'sad' enough already without me making it worse. Remember it's not personal, drive on.

Retailers and shop owners can find themselves also in the line for misplaced aggression. I can remember in my days of retailing timber almost coming to 'blows' with irrate customers.

A customer is always right. So the saying goes! Again in modern society people want things there and now. No waiting, no excuses, no being 'fobbed off'. If they think they are they will 'go into one'. Beware of the building signs of disgruntlment and try to nip them in the bud. To not add fuel to the fire by aurgueing back or being sarcastic, it makes things worse.

Believe me I speak from experience.

But remember you are not paid to be abused or assaulted. So if you feel you are in danger, leave and get some one else in higher authority to deal with the problem. Do not be bullied or intimidated. These people will do it, they will threaten your life in some instances to get their way. Fore-warned is fore-armed. I feel every retail business should have conflict management courses to educate their staff on how to cope with aggressive customers.

I am sure that you, the reader, can now think of upteen situations where you have wondered 'What's the matter with this person, why are they so angry and aggressive at me for such a small reason?' Now you know. Misplaced aggression.

In the settings of the social scene (pubs, night clubs, bars) watch out for the above mentioned people, they are there tuning in on you enjoying yourself. Because they are not having much fun in their lives they will take offence that you are. They will stand at a distance observing and gradually talking themselves into the convincing conclusion in their minds that you will have to experience some of their pain. That they will have to wipe the smile off of your face. How dare you enjoy yourself infront of them! They will work themselves up to boiling point and then approach you with menacing intent. Be warned they will not think twice about trying to alter your features with a beer glass or bottle. In their miserable, twisted minds you deserve it.

These individuals will stand and watch people and if they see a likely candidate to unload their resentment and rage upon, they will act.

Here are some of the reasons and dialogue that may lead up to your encounter. They have watched you and come to some conclusion:

a) Look at that p ---- k! He thinks he's some sort of fashion model wearing a

suit like that and those shoes. Flash git. Well I'll soon put him straight.

b) What's he doing with a gorgeous babe like that? What does she see in him? He's a pratt, just look at him. What a tosser. He thinks he's God's gift , I'll show him!

c) That bastards too happy, look at him. Centre of attention, spinning some bullshit story just to impress the crowd. I'll bloody have him!

You see, you can't predic t what will set this person off but to rest assured something will do the job. Once they have justified their actions in their minds then not much will stop them carrying out their act of retribution. Jealousy and pain in a person's life can lead them to do all sorts of crazy things, even murder!

Alcohol in this sort of environment can fuel their aggression but we cannot blame it. Some people can become mellow and happy when they have a drink and are no trouble. Others go the opposite way, but 1 believe it has to be in them anyway to do these terrible thing to others. Alcohol is just the catalyst and later becomes the excuse. Like the husband who batters his wife after having got drunk. He then blames it on the alcohol. What a load of rubbish, that is a cop out. It's in their nature and alcohol just spured it on.

1 hope this chapter makes clear the problems and unpredictability of misplaced aggression and you are more aware of the causes.

Chapter 9 'Ego'

'His ego entered the room 10 minutes before the rest of him!'

In our youth dealing with your ego can be a big problem. You are at an age when you are out to prove exactly who you are and be accepted into certain circles. Between 15 and 25 years of age we live with the ego everyday. Although I must admit I have met some 40 and 50 year olds that are still struggling with theirs! (poor sods!)

Peer pressure as a young man will convince you that you have to act in a macho way to be accepted. You can be brain washed into acts of aggression and violence because you feel this is what is expected of you. This is the basis that a lot of gang culture is built on and it's all part of 'belonging'.

In this world people can be split into two groups, Alpha's and Betas. The Alpha person is a leader, a hunter gatherer. Somebody who likes to be in charge and in control.

The Beta person is a follower, they are more subservient and consequently more likely to be led than to be a leader.

In the animal kingdom this is also true. You have a dominant Alpha male who leads the herd and controls it. His authority and leadership is not questioned. The rest accept and follow him. They are the Beta group.

Now trouble will appear when another dominant Alpha male intrudes on the herd and decides it wants leadership. Then both males will posture, roar, stamp, strut, whatever the ritual of aggression is they will show. If this doesn't work and no one backs down a fight for supremacy will begin. This accurately mirrors two human males, when their ego's won't back down. They will feel they have to met the challenge. Hold eye contact, gesture, posture, spout abuse. The signs and rituals are all there leading up to physical violence. Within certain gangs and groups it's the done thing, it is expected. You don't back down, you don't look for compromise, you just wade in and start punching.

The individual can be spurred on by his 'mates'. Drumming into him that he's being taken for a mug, wouldn't stand for that, show him who he's dealing with! This all adds fuel to the fire and stokes the aggression and testoserone levels.

1 have known many dangerous individuals with big ego's. They will not walk away from trouble. They will instigate it and make it happen. They will not be told what to do. They just can't live with this. Some will immediately explode and be volatile, others will let their feelings fester away and build up until they have thought of a way to get their own back. Revenge is a by-product of ego. These people can be unpredictable and dangerous.

If you have a confrontation with them, they may suddenly back off telling you it's all a mistake. But as soon as your back is turned or your guard is lowered they will attack.

Ego can be the cause of some horrific violence perpetrated by men and woman alike.

Fights that develop over females are usually ego based. The old chestnut 'Are you looking at my bird?' Is always a good start point! All of us men are guilty of being protective towards our ladies but we have got to learn to think with our heads and not our fists!

The male ego can be a fragile thing especially where women are concerned. Many situations have developed from one person eyeing up or talking to another man's lady. The trouble is even the most mild manner male suddenly turns into 'the Terminator' when his lady is insulted or threatened. Most ladies will brush it off and forget a situation, not the males. No they are in there full steam ahead with 'Have you got a problem pal?' etc, etc.

Remember earlier we spoke about icy and fiery aggression, this is the classic case of fiery. No fore thought, no plan, just walk straight in to trouble.

Recall the snappy put downs and one liners that were used earlier on, well here's the chance to exercise them. Be smart. Use your head. Be the one in control, not the one being controlled.

If you are walking down the street and a gang of youths shouted out 'w--k-r' in your direction most probably you would walk on and ignore it. After all why get involved with 4 or 5 people? This is a dangerous thing to do. Had you been walking with your girlfriend or wife and suddenly you have become 'Sir Gallihad', Clint Eastwood and Russell Crowe rolled into one! You will retaliate, feeling your manhood threatened. That macho-man programming that you have had fed to you for years kicks in and off you go to wade into dangerous waters and in most cases you are likely to drown!

Grow up, get real. Remember an insult is a word or words to get a certain response. Forget it, don't play the game. Rise above it. Walk on it's nothing personal. If you are called a 'Hairy arsed moron' why let it bother, you unless you are one! If not, walk on, water off a duck's back. Keep the ego under check. This is the best way to respond.

In my back ground of Martial Arts I have met some fantastic people. Dedicated, talented and humble individuals who sum up what Martial Arts are about. They have the exceptional ability to be able to defend themselves without a problem. These people are 'the real deal', they do not have to prove anything, they don't need to, they are totally devoid of ego. A person for an example like Karate legend and Self Protection pioneer Peter Consterdine has the awesome power to kill with his hands and feet. Do you think that is an exaggeration? Then please go train with him and find out. His striking power is something others can only dream of and probably never achieve. Now think of the confidence you must process when you have that skill. Yet Peter is constantly striving to better his self all the time plus he is one of the most humble people you can meet for all his talent and experience he is willing to learn from others not as highly qualified as himself. Plus he has always got time to talk to you, not at you which is a big difference. Geoff Thompson, Neil Adams, Rick Young and so many others are of the same nature. Yet on the other side of the coin I have met certain characters whose ego's come into a room 10 minutes before the rest of them! If they booked a seat on a plane it would have to be one for themselves and one next door for the ego!

These people have self imposed themselves onto heady pedestals and actually are legends in their own minds! Fancy titles before their names, high Dan grade rankings and Gi's (training suit) with their names emblazoned on the back seem to make them think they are God almighty. Whether they actually have ability is besides the point because unfortunately they come over as self important big headed arseholes!

They will tell you their life history within 5 minutes of meeting you. Impress on you how deadly their skills are and why their system is the best and every one else's is crap. They will strut around like an over stuffed peacock with piles, correcting your every move with an air of arrogance as if you should be grateful that they spared you their time. To say these people take themselves too seriously, is an under statement. I won't name names save embarrassment but if I ever got like that I would tell my students to put me out of my misery!

You can tell this is one of my pet hates and one I try not to let get to me but sometimes I digress, we are all human!

I remember something Geoff Thompson said to me on one occasion. *'If you don't want to associate with arseholes, don't go to where arseholes hang out'* Oh so true.

I have learnt to dispel my ego and my self inflated opinion of myself years ago. I did this through hard training and a lot of self analysis.

Training wise I have never hid behind my grade or title. Throwing a complient partner all over the place when teaching can look absolutely wonderful but let's not kid ourselves it's like that in the 'real world'.

Putting yourself on the line and pressure testing your skills will deflate the ego, especially when you get beat!

Regularly I still box, wrestle, kick box and train Vale Tudo (no holds barred) sparring and fighting with my fellow instructors and students. The belt is disregarded and I have a go. I am not frightened of the outcome because I am confident I can hold my own. I don't profess to be a master or the world's best Martial Artist, but what I can say is I can and will give it a go in any arena. I am not worried about my grade, reputation or status. Only ego lets you worry about those things!

I have competed in many mixed arenas even recently fighting in full contact Vale Tudo type contest at the age of 40 and still gave as good as I got! I don't say this to boast, I say it to illustrate I am still prepared to learn and test myself. I also realise there are many talented young Martial Artists on their way up the ranks who are going to be awesome. I live in a world of reality not some over-hyped dream world where I am the ultimate warrior!

Ironically by having done the things I have, Ihave gained more respect and reputation from students and fellow instructors because they see at least I practise what I preach.

People who have worked to control their ego don't need to strut around snarling and growling telling you how dangerous they are. When individuals tell me this I wonder who they are trying to convince, me or themselves? Ego means insecurity and doubt. That's why said persons have to go around persuading you how great they are!

I could fill a few chapters telling you of my training, ability and exploits but hey so could another 100 better Martial Artists. Who cares? It's easy to hit somebody, the hardest job is walking away from trouble. That's when you know you are a true warrior not a power ranger!

Avoid pointless arguments or wasting your breath slagging somebody off. Do something more productive with your time, you will feel better. Too many people are walking around with the burden of hate, revenge and ego on their back's. Try and lighten the load. No, its not easy, I am working every day but I know I am heading in the right direction. I can't even remember the last time I had an argument with someone. Yet a few years back it was becoming a daily accurance, I don't miss it at all.

I think of the ego as a 'little demon' in a bottle. If you keep that cork in the bottle you won't have a problem. Sometimes you may hear the demon begging to be released or banging on the glass, but don't be persuaded to 'uncork' it otherwise you will have a job to get it back in the bottle! I tend to think of anger or aggression as the same, very rarely these days do I 'uncork' either but if I do I always know I have enough control to redirect the 'demon' back to it's bottle!

'if he went to school without his boots, it was because he was too big for them ' Quote.

Chapter 10
Fighters come in many guises

When you hear the word 'Fighter' mentioned, who does it conjure images up of in your mind? The legendary Bruce Lee perhaps? Ali or Tyson? Rickson Gracie? Maybe Marco Ruas or the late 'Guv'nor, Lennie Mc Lean? The list is endless, it can go on and on depending on how you interpret the question.

The term fighter can transcend just the physical attributes of a person. Being big, having your head shaved and investing in a few evil looking tattoos or some radical body piercing does not make you a 'hard' man, nor does wearing a T-shirt with the Gracic Ju Jutsu Academy logo emblazoned on it, for example!

These outward images can sometimes mean nothing whatsoever, they can be masking inner weaknesses. Please don't confuse big and strong with tough, they can be totally different things, as outlined in my book, *'I thought you'd be bigger. A small person's guide to fighting back'* and Jamie O'Keefe's text *'What makes tough guys tough?'*

In my job as a Martial Arts/Self Protection instructor, I have come across guys who really 'look the part' as fighters but when push comes to shove they melted inside like an ice lolly in the sun! I have encountered others you would not take a second glance at who have been ferocious fighters with bags of courage and determination. Pumping a few weights and learning to throw a few punches is not what it's all about. As my good friend and fellow Martial Artist Geoff Thompson would say 'rather 20 stone of mental muscle up here in the mind than on the 'biceps'?

The key attributes of a real fighter are mental toughness, undying resolve and iron will. These things can see you through most situations and help you to survive. Take for example members of the S.A.S. arguably the elite of the world's fighting forces. With the training they endure, and the feats they have achieved in battle, you would think they were monsters of men but in reality they could walk past you in the street and you would not afford them a second glance, yet these men are fierce fighters of the highest level. It's their mental toughness and incredible iron will that drives them through some of the most adverse situations. Look at Andy Mc Nab, author of 'Bravo Two Zero' and the torture and hardship he suffered at the hands of the Iraqis and he lived to tell the tale - this man is a true Fighter.

I have just read a book called 'Soldiers and Sherpas' by another ex S.A.S. man called 'Brummie' Stokes, not only did he face many adverse situations in some of the most dangerous parts of the world serving in the forces, he also was an avid climber who conquered the south face of Mount Everest. During that time he witnessed four of his friends fall to their deaths and was himself buried for 3 days under an avalanche of snow, as well as having all his toes amputated after severe frostbite. After 6 months he was back with the S.A.S. taking 85 mile hikes across the Brecon Beacons and 5 years later returned to Everest to climb the north face! A story of unbelievable courage, savage determination and a true fighter's spirit. This man achieved and endured things others can only sit and imagine in their wildest dreams or nightmares.

On his final assault on the north-east ridge of Everest he sustained a fractured neck after being caught in another avalanche and having to travel two days before getting to hospital for treatment! What an inspirational story it was!

As was the book the Diving Bell and the Butterfly by Jean Dominique Bauby. The author suffered a massive stroke leaving him with the rare 'locked in syndrome'. His brain was functioning perfectly but he was completely paralysed and speechless, only able to move one eyelid. With his eyelid he 'dictated' remarkable book, is this man not a 'Fighter?' You see that this inner strength can be a great source of belief and survival. Take Evander Holyfield the former world heavyweight boxing champion, a man who not only has the physical attributes of a world class fighter but also the incredible inner strength to go with it.

The legendary modern day explorer Sir Ralph Fiennes who walked across the frozen wastes of Antartica amongst many other great adventures is a man of extreme mental and physical toughness. He has literally stared death in the face and carried right on.

Mike Stroud author of 'Survival of the fittest', is another man of incredible indurance and tenacity. You would have to be especially tough to run a 130 mile marathon across the blazing heat of the Sahara Desert.

These people come in all shapes, sizes and ages. Helen Klein a 72 year old grandmother entered the first Eco-challenge race in Utah USA. This is a 300 mile race through demanding back country. The ways to cross this distance were different disciplines, one after the other. Running, hiking, mountain biking, horse riding, canoeing, white water rafting and rock climbing. She completed the course beating people half her age. What an amazing resolve to push herself through the pain barrier.

Toughness goes far beyond physical fighting skills. The local neighbourhood or pub 'hardcase' is not in these people's league when it come to 'real' toughness. Some so called 'hard men' are two a penny, these aforementioned people and others like them are a rare breed.

Is Mike Tyson a fighter? In one sense of the word undoubtedly. But look at the weakness of his character outside the ring and the crazy and sad things that he has brought upon himself. 1 am not preaching here, I have made my fair share of mistakes and can be ferociously tough in some aspects of my life and then weak in others, I constantly strive to address the balance but many people can't even see or begin to admit when they have weaknesses.

The individuals I have mentioned and many more like them are a constant source of inspiration and true fighters. We can draw courage and enlightenment from these people to reach our own personal goals and overcome hardships or mental barriers in our lives.

As Martial Artists you can come up against many pitfalls and hurdles that mentally challenge us all. Whether it be winning or competing in a tournament, passing a grading, surviving a tough grappling session or getting through a tough exercise or workout session. Each time you do this, you can become mentally stronger and in turn push towards your goals as a 'fighter'. When you feel stale or deflated, draw inspiration from others that have overcome adversity in their lives and achieved greater goals.

I was greatly inspired when I first read 'Watch my Back' by Geoff Thompson and can still be inspired by it many years later when I read it. When meeting Geoff and talking to him, he never fails to inspire me. People can slag' off Geoff or disagree with what he says but I defy anybody not to be inspired in this man's company, it takes a special person to do this.

Recently Geoff came to my home town of Bristol to promote his latest books and gave a talk and book signing at Waterstones Bookstore one evening. Geoff spoke for over two hours and I must emphasize not just about himself. As the employees of the shop were cleaning up and locking up, Geoff still had his audience enthralled (although his wife Sharon was tapping her watch in the background to remind him it had been a long day!). Geoff patiently waited and spoke to and signed copies of his books for all who were there and had time to pose for a few photographs. He is a true 'pro' and a man who can inspire you to 'get off your butt' and achieve your goals. He has made a great many people do this, me included!

As stated 'Fighters' come in many shapes and sizes and most importantly, moulds. Some people who know nothing about a right cross or a roundhouse kick can have tremendous reserve of mental strength that some so called 'Fighters' could never obtain.

Another person who has to be mentioned in the category of a fighter and a truly inspirational person is Paddy Doyle - holder of numerous titles for feats of unbelievable fitness and endurance. This man's mental capacity to push himself to new and higher levels of achievement through adversity must be admired.

I have a constant source of inspiration to me closer to home, it's my mother . Some years ago she suffered a massive stroke that left her partially paralysed down her left side. My mother was to say the very least an incredibly active woman. From my childhood to very recently, I remember her running around constantly, cooking, cleaning, caring for her family and many many others, it was her life.

When she suffered the stroke it must have devastated her. Initially she could hardly move, could not feed herself and had speech difficulty and many other problems; but through intense physiotherapy and a tough daily, regime of personal exercises, she has made immense steps back to full health. She still has no use of her arm but she has retrained herself to walk, she can talk fine and do most things on her own and her mind is as sharp as ever.

I can say it was her undying fighting spirit, determination and will to survive that helped her achieve this - I honestly believe a lesser person would be dead by now. She is a shining example of a true 'fighter' and a continuing source of inspiration every time I go to visit her .

Realise the true measure of a fighter is the heart and his will to survive - outward appearances can be deceiving, you can't always judge a book by its cover!

Finally no truer saying can there be than *'When the going gets tough, the tough get going'*

Chapter 11
'Size isn't Everything'
'Dont mistake size for toughness'

In my very first book, 'I thought you'd be bigger' - A small person's guide to fighting back'. I went into great detail about facing a large adversary and how to defend yourself, also I spoke about the psychological side of how we preceive big aggressive people and the barriers that we have to remove before we can even hope of thinking we can fight back against them if the occasion arises.

I would like to in this chapter go over some of those points and also cover some new territory on this subject.

Personally I was brought up on the idea that the bigger you were the tougher you had to be. My comic book hero's were all huge characters. The films portrayed every hero as being big and strong types. John Wayne, Clint Eastwood, Swarzenegger, Stallone and so on. No small guys apart from the legendary Bruce Lee ever was the famous screen hero.

At school the big, strong lads were always selected for sports, the smaller mostly over looked. In the play ground the bully nine times out of ten was bigger than you. The mental programming was embedded in my subconscious, So I had to begin to reprogramme my thoughts. Bruce Lee made me do this at the age of fourteen. I saw this small man of tremendously conditioned but light frame perform some amazing things and it began to make me see things in a different light. But it wasn't an overnight transformation.

No it took many years to lose the programming of big is better.

I learnt that a lot of big guys actually hated their size because it did make them a target for trouble because everybody persumed they could handle themselves. I can remember attending a seminar a few years ago hosted by the late, great Gary Spiers (Gary had some 30+ years in frontline security and faced countless life threatening situations) I recall him saying that a lot of smaller guys he worked with ' on doors' would comment that they wished they had his size (20+ stone). Gary replied, 'No you don't'. See when trouble comes you can run and squeeze out through a toilet window and escape. Me I'm so big I have to stand and face the music!' I haven't got much choice' I must say here that although I didn't know Gary personally his untimely death sent shock waves through the Martial Arts world and a void that I don't think will ever be filled. He was a larger than life character, a ferocious fighter but a man of honour. He was a big man who could certainly talk the talk and walk the walk!

I have met many a 'gentle giant' in my travels that are true gentlemen and found they were purely targeted for their size. I have trained a few that look very imposing but have a great lack of confidence and self belief and hate the fact that people look upon them as a threat.

Yet others use their size to intimidate and bully. They show excessive aggression and attempt to impose themselves on people by using their belief that big means tough! As mentioned most people are programmed to believe just that, that's why they get away with it!

I have trained in gyms most of my life using weights etc. I have met some smashing people in these places also I have run across some complete a-h --- s! You know the guys that snarl and glare when you enter a gym. They strut around arms splayed as if carrying two buckets of water! They give you you the evil eye, the hard stare. What's that all about? Why do I always feel in some training gyms everybody is looking for a fight with you. They are all under the illusion that because they can hunk some huge poundages of 'iron' around that they are 'fighters'. Forget it, it doesn't always translate. Some are and some aren't!

1 have boxed, wrestled and free sparred guys twice my size who didn't have any fighting ability at all. Once you survived their initial burst of aggression they tired quicker than a 'big tired thing' and were easy to handle.

Thinking you are a fighter and being one is two different things and the space between both is a vast chasm!

I have seen guys 'working the doors' that have got by for years on the pure buff of size and having some front. When it actually come to the physical and they weren't throwing out some totally legless young student, they had pitiful fighting ability. No balance, no timing, no power, no control. They had got by on the myth that their size was enough.

This maybe the case if a person isn't willing to step over the line with you and try you out. But there are some people out there who don't care about your size or how much you can bench press! They will step over the line and some of these 'sugar coated tough guys' will crumble to dust. Please don't assume by lifting a few weights and punching a bag now and then is enough. To be a true fighter unless you are naturally gifted you will have to work long and hard to achieve.

Now don't get me wrong when a big skilled fighter meets a little skilled fighter , 9 times out of 10 the big man will win. But that is skilled fighters not 'wannabe's'.

I have found when big guys confront smaller ones, they are over-confident in the belief they couldn't possibly be beat. This over confidence and arrogance can be their down fall if they get too cocky. Once more as the average smaller person is led to believe that they couldn't possibly beat a bit guy. The big guy is programmed to believe that they couldn't possibly lose to a small man.

You need to review and reprogramme your thoughts on this subject. Just as I mentioned that you would view a guy with a shaven skull and tatooes as dangerous, because thats how they have always been portrayed, you may find he's anything but dangerous.

Remember a lot of animals will puff up their plummage, expand their skin, blow out their bodies in many weird and wonderful ways to ward off prospective enemies, so to will humans. But behind all this there may be nothing else. Of course you have got to have the 'bottle' to have a look. That can be the hardest thing.

Here is an extract from my book, 'I thought you'd be bigger', to help you understand about the ways you can mentally reprogramme yourself ....

This confidence comes through training in proper combat techniques that suit your build and stature. As you progress and learn the feeling of control and confidence, your abilities will develop.

Remember though never be brash, arrogant or big headed and don't underestimate anyone. Just channel that burning inner feeling of how to cope with a violent and dangerous encounter if it happens.

After self-belief you must learn to build ruthless determination. The next essential ingredient. Once you decide on defending yourself you must go at it a 100%. All thoughts of defeat, injury and pain to your own self must be blotted out and never enter your mind.

If you let these thoughts enter your mind, you will lose the confrontation. You have to keep on fighting like a savage animal until the attacker is incapable of further action. Don't hold back - see that he is stopped.

The law forbids you to take revenge but it permits you to prevent. Do what you have to do to prevent the assault. Let's face it your attacker is not going to be worried about your welfare. If he is physically bigger and stronger you must not allow him the chance to get into the fight. You may only get one chance so make it count, swarm and overwhelm your opponent.

If you get punched, kicked, grabbed, keep fighting! Don't let the mind give in; as soon as it does you will be beaten. Most fights finish because one of the participants has mentally given up, not necessarily because of their physical injuries.

If after you receive a few blows let your mind say 'this hurts, I will defeat you no matter what!'

This sort of determined outlook will give you a distinct psychological edge; it will also give you the advantage to win!

Remember a big huy who chooses to attack you is 100% sure he can beat you. His physique is I'm bigger so I'm better. He sees you as no threat and doesn't believe you can harm him. Blow his stupid and over confident attitude out of the window along with his senses. Turn into that pit bull; blitz him from all angles with blows. Overwhelm him with sheer desire to win and ruthless fury. Make him suddenly think what the hell have I taken on here?

Can you recall a part in the film 'Jurassic Park' when the guy who stole the dinosaur embryos was trying to get away, when he was confronted by what looked like a small playful dinosaur? Him believing so, didn't treat it with the respect it deserved. Then suddenly it turned into a ferocious, poison spitting, man-eating nightmare!

By the time the guy realised what he was up against it was too late! Get the idea, remember how people might perceive you then prove them wrong.

You see psychologically you have turned the tables. There's nothing worse than when a supremely confident fighter suddenly finds himself on the receiving end of punishment rather than dishing it out! Some don't know how to handle it and won't be able to re-a-just quickly enough.

So cultivate this mindset and show no fear, even if your stomach is churning over inside, channel the feeling positively, except them and make them work for you. Wear the mask of a cold and calculating veteran of many such battles. Stare at your opponent with blank, expressionless eyes, like shark's eyes, pull your lips back in a grim determined smile. All these tactics will unnerve your attacker.

Think again how the pit bull will have no hesitation or fear when attacking a larger dog than itself.

That's because it has an inner belief in itself and a will to win, so can you!

Another component to the whole picture is developing a 'killer instinct!' This is the ability basically to finish the fight, to resoundingly defeat your attacker.

You must strive for this, make no mistake your attacker given the chance will finish you, whether it be beat you, stab you or kick you to a pulp!

The days of fair play are gone, the hardened mugger or psycho street fighter will not worry about stooping to the lowest level to beat you. Unfortunately you may have to stoop even lower to defeat them!

But remember you are doing this for a different motive than them, you are doing it to defend yourself, your family, your loved ones, whatever the case maybe.

You must have no compulsion to going in and ruthlessly finishing the fight, do not let them off 'the hook' you may not get a second chance.

Once they realise you can look after yourself and the essential element of surprise is gone, they will up the stakes and the intensity of their assault, so finish it!

You may say it's not in your nature to be aggressive and that you despise violence. 1 also hate violence if it can be avoided then fine,, but sometimes it comes knocking at your door and you can't hide from it.

Then you have got to summon up courage and defiance and fight back.

Today's society unfortunately is a violent one, robbery, rape, muggings, murder, kidnapping and terrorism, down to road rage and domestic squabbles. Today's street fighter or thug is different from yesteryear. He may come into the confrontation totally 'crazed' on booze, pills, or drugs.

Nine times out of ten probably armed or 'carrying' he is a biter, a gouger and a stamper, he will not back off when you hit the floor, he will carry on stomping and kicking.

He is a psychopath. You cannot plead to his good or moral side, he hasn't got one, he is an animal, make no mistake.

So when the chips are down and it's you or him who is going to survive, it has to be you, no question!

The killer instinct can be switched on or off at will.

it can lie dormant inside you as you go about your everyday life but when trouble looms you can switch it on instantly. 1 liken it to having a monster inside you that every now and then you will let off the lease to have the run of the place. But when the job is done it is chained safely back up again. You must never let the monster escape or control you; you must be its master and have control of it at all times. To hope to control another person you must first control yourself!

All these fighting components must come under the heading of 'fighting spirit', or controlled aggression.

Never anger, rage, or out of control. It's not about letting the 'red mist' come over the eyes and 'loosing it'.

In that case you will use precious energy up with no result, you will blindly wade in to deeper troubled water and finally drown!

Look at some of the World Class boxers in their prime like Mike Tyson, Marvin Hagler, Duran, Leonard, Benn.

When their opponent was in trouble, when they sensed victory they were in there and took the opponent out the game but although it was ferocious it was still controlled and when it was done they switched it off.

Former World Middle weight champion Marvin Hagler had a fearsome reputation in the ring and was a terrific finisher but outside the ring was said to be a quietly spoken gentleman.

This is what you must strive for, if these boxers forementioned had hesitated in those crucial times it would have cost them their titles and a fortune of money. If you hesitate it may cost you a higher price, your life!

You can have all the best fighting moves in the world but if you haven't developed the right mental attitude it is like having a handful of bullets but with no gun to fire them!

The techniques are a hollow shell without emotional content.

If you still doubt your ability to develop these attributes then quietly sit down for a moment and visualise your worst nightmare. For instant being held at knife point and being forced to watch your wife being raped or your children beaten.

Visualise now some faceless fiend that you fear pulling up in a car outside. He's huge, aggressive and has a reputation for hurting people. He's now walking up your drive. The doorbell rings and you unexpectedly answer the door and he pushes his way in. Your wife is in the kitchen, your kids asleep upstairs. What are you going to do?

Can you honestly now say you cannot conjure up the necessary mindset needed to survive? Of course you can, you have no choice.

If by even reading these words they have conjured up feelings of fear, repulsion, nausea, panic, then take the opportunity to channel these feelings positively to fight back and win!

Fear is natural, everybody gets it, and it's how you control it that's the key. Under pressure you will get the 'fight or flight' syndrome! The body is preparing and priming itself for confrontation, it is a primitive animal, survival tactic that dates right back to the beginning of time.

Don't be frightened, if you have to fight it will initially powerhouse your body and give you super charged strength and speed but it won't last long until you will get the down side of the adrenaline rush, exhaustion.

Most live confrontations will happen quickly and not last long, so channel the adrenaline into a burst of controlled aggression and take your assailant out.

More about the bodies functioning under stress later. When you carry the right mental attitude you will surprise the larger assailant and defeat him. But you must have belief in yourself that you can do it. What you lack in physical size make up with the heart of a lion!

Chapter 12
'Are you looking at me?'
Predicting signs of aggression

In the course of your everyday routines the chances of having to deal with an aggressive individual may vary with your circumstances. Anybody may be the victim of a road rage out burst when they are going about their regular travels. In the working environment you may have to deal with irrate customersAs a manager or supervisor you will probably somewhere along the way have to deal with angry staff members. As a school teacher you may have to handle situations with aggressive or abusive pupils. In your personal life perhaps you have to manage the aggression of a partner or family member or friend. The list can be endless. It can vary from disagreements to shouting matches right up to physical and verbal abuse. If you work in the line of security, doorwork, police etc you may have to deal with some pretty nasty situations, it goes with the territory, so to speak. But then again nurses and doctors in a busy A.E department will also encounter their fair share of violence. As mentioned before violence and aggression can materialise everywhere, anytime. Crimes are no longer perpetrated under the cover of darkness. The thugs have come out of the shadows and will now operate in the day light hours.

It will serve us all well to be able to see and predict the signs of violence and aggression well before they escalate into physical attacks.

If you have to confront a person and attempt to calm them down and reason with them, watch out for these early warning signals that they are not happy with your approach or what you are saying.

Sighing, looking away, avoiding eye contact, finger tapping, lint picking (picking imaginary fluff from clothing), rubbing earlobe or head, lop sided grin, arms folded, hands on hips, shaking head.

If you see these above signs developing try and adjust your approach and put the ball back in their court by saying something like 'It's obvious you don't agree with what I'm saying, so tell me what you think'. Do not pursue a negative line of conversation or attempt to be-little an individual otherwise it will force him to become more aggressive and dangerous. Remember there are ways of conversing to hopefully calm situations, there are also other methods that will aggravate a person and make them more aggitated.

I have found some people in authority will talk down to others and try to humiliate another. Because of their 'position of power' they believe they can get away with this and go through life talking to everybody like this. They feel their status has made them 'bullet proof' and they ignore the danger signs until it's too late.

Many years ago as a young man I saw my boss punched out because he handled a situation with a customer wrongly. As I mentioned in the building trade you can meet some pretty volatile characters. My boss tried to belittle this person in front of others and paid the price! But unfortunately he didn't learn his lesson, most never do!

If you don't see these warning signals mentioned or choose to ignore them they will move on to a second level, as follows:Fast pacing and irractic movement, voice raising (shouting or threatening), eye balling, fixed starting, invading of personal space, heavy breathing, opening and closing of hands, blood red neck/face, veins protruding in neck/temple, swearing/cursing, finger pointing, finger wagging, insults (e.g. finger tapping head 'your mad,' circling finger by head, 'nutter', 'v' sign, middle finger, or circle with thumb/fore finger.

At this stage you are in danger of being physically assaulted, this will be the next and final level.

You must start thinking about protecting your personal space and keeping distance between you and your aggressor. Do not let them get inside your arms length. Let's examine our spacial zones and observe how we feel when people are at varying distances from us. Personal Territory The area most animals will defend are the zone around the body. The nest of their young and the territory they feed in or roam in. When these areas are threatened as examined earlier on, the animal will posture and become aggressive as they sense danger.

We are no different. We like to feel dominant in our home surroundings, car, office space etc. Some people are prepared to fight to the death to claim their parking space. We like to show ownership of personal belongings or indeed out loved ones. These are subtle warning signals to others to back off. When we get a door to door sales person come around and we don't feel comfortable with them we will hold the door half open or lean on the door frame to block the entrance. These are small sublimal gestures to let them know we are wary of them.

Here is how we react in certain personal zones:

1) Public zone (12ft) - It is a distance we may address an audience or group of people, if speaking. The people and ourselves will feel comfortable here.

2) Social zone (4-12ft) - This zone can be seen in the street or shops. Shop assistants, business people, clients will all work in this zone.

3) Personal zone (1ft 6ins - 4ft) - Most western people will stand at this distance in social gatherings or occasions like parties or social functions. This is a comfortable distance to talk to new acquaintances.

4) Intimate zone (6ins-1ft 6ins) - This zone is reserved for close friends, relatives and loved ones. A stranger coming into this zone is certainly a threat. When we are sat on a crowded bus or stood on a busy tube we may have to endure people who we don't know this close to us. When this happens we go into our own 'space bubbles' and try not to make eye contact with the other person and remain staring out of a window. You can feel quite uncomfortable in this situation, even claustrophobic. In large crowds of people you can also feel this way especially at large events like football matches, theme parks or music concerts. I feel like this every time I visit London and walk down Oxford Street and have also experienced this in the USA, places like New York and San Francisco.

5) Close Intimate zone (0-15cms -0-6ins) - Normally reserved for a lover. This is a private and personal zone. Normally anybody else that violates this zone will do so for violent or sexual reasons. At this range when a stranger gets this close our bodies go under chemical changes to prepare for un wanted attention or worse.

The final conclusion to this escalating threat will be physical contact if you haven't successfully controlled your personal space and talked this aggressor down. There are some excellent books on handling this type of situation. Geoff Thompson's excellent texts 'The Fence' and '3 second fighter' by Summerdale go into great detail on this subject as to does Jamie O'Keefe's 'Pre-emptive strikes for winning fights' by New Breed. At the final stage the aggressor will possibly prod you in the chest with a finger, start rapid pushing with their finger tips, large explosive pushing, swinging a punch, head butt or kick, grabbing and grappling you or using some type of weapon against you.

We are now into the realms of close quarter fighting and you would do well to read my books, 'I'd thought you'd be bigger, 'In your Face' and 'Grappling with Reality' to get a full picture on this side of things. All are published by New Breed.

This is where you want to avoid going to, but sometimes all else will fail and you will have to physically fight back or be badly hurt or worse. When these violent people start they will attack quickly and viciously and won't stop. If you go down they will kick and stomp all over you until they are satisfied. Pleading isn't going to help.

I was once asked what is the best self defence technique and I replied not to be there when trouble begins and I hold by this.

When you gain an understanding of the type of person that instigates violence and the various signs, signals and rituals they will use hopefully you will have avoided any trouble before it ever 'kicks off'. This is the whole theme of this book. If you are in a jungle and hear a lion roar you beat a hasty retreat not go searching for it!

We all have built in survival instincts that can alert us to impending dangers. For instance we wouldn't want to swim in the sea with a red flag flying on the beach or if the waters were suspected of being shark infested! Just as we shouldn't drive without a seat belt, pick up hitch hikers, take a short cut across a dark common to get home. Yet with all our built in survival signals we do all the above things. Why?

It all boils down to the fact that although we know the dangers we are in a state of denial. 'It won't happen to me' syndrome. When the acceptance of danger is not present we will not see a situation develop until it is far too late. Nobody wants to believe anything nasty can happen to them, but we have got to have acceptance that it can and will if we are not switched on and clued up..

Another excellent book that explores this topic in great detail is Peter Consterdine's 'Streetwise,' Protection publications.

What you have to get used to is the fact nobody is immune to violence. No matter your age, sex, colour, status, you can be a victim.

Violence can happen anywhere, even in the most unlightly of places. It's not just reserved for the proverbial dark alley.

It will depend on what circles you move in. It will determine the percentage of likelihood to accounting violence. The age groups that are most vunerable are probably 16 to 25 year olds and over 60's. Why? At 16 to 25 you move in social circles of pubs, clubs and night life. Surroundings involving alcohol and to certain extents drugs, all will fuel violence. I suspect everybody at this age has encountered some sort of physical violence.

The elderly are also targets for muggers and thieves. Whether it be along the streets having their purses snatched or con-men gaining false entry into their homes they become victims.

The places you inhabit or the circles you move in can also up the chances of facing aggression. It's up to you to decide what you want to do. Either you begin to change your lifestyle or accept you will be in a higher bracket of unreliability to face violence. Like I said we all can be victims but the idea of good self protection is to narrow down the odds. It's the same principle if you were concerned about security for your house. If you rang up the crime protection officer and ask for suggestions on how to make you feel more secure in your premises against burglers and he replied. 'Get yourself a baseball bat and keep it by your bedside!' You may not be looking for something so final. He may suggest security lights, window locks, an alarm system, you would be building barriers to make burglary more difficult. The baseball bat would be your very last option when all other security measures have failed. It's the same with personal self protection, let's strive to do everything we can to avoid the physical.

A good self protection teacher will be teaching 95% avoidance and 5% physical. Most so call 'self defence' teachers are teaching this back to front!

If you go back to house security, the police will tell you if you want to know if your house is secure, look at it from a burglars point of view. Or if you forget your front door key could you still get in somewhere? When you have done this, then start cutting out the options, until there are none left.

The same again applies to personal self defence. You have to analyse your daily life and routines and see if you are vunerable to violence, if so then start adjusting to cut down the options.

No two peoples lives are the same. Obviously if you are the PM or a member of royalty your security will be different to the average man or woman as your threat assessment will be higher. Never the less you can still apply the same principles.

Some professions carry high risk as we spoke about earlier. Or if you are a business man that travels regularly to foreign countries you will need to be clued up on their customs and ways.

For instance I can remember attending a seminar with lsraeli Krav Maga expert Eyal Yanilov, who has trained Army, Security, and Civilians for jobs all over the world. He mentioned that modes of violence differ in various parts of the world. In South America he said muggers will always operate in two's and usually in broad day light. One will come up to you and press a gun into your belly while another will approach from the blind side and take your wallet. Slick, fast and professional. Another method for you to be approached by is from the front and asked a pretty innocuous question and again another mugger would come from the back and put a knife to your throat.

Violence can also be more extreme in some countries and that's the norm for them. It may be shocking to us but acceptable in some foreign parts.

Remember the other year in Turkey when Leeds United fans were stabbed to death in fights with Galatasseri supporters? It was shocking and the tabloids ran stories about the so called 'Turkish animals and maniacs'.

I don't for one minute condone what happened. But knife culture is the normal fighting technique in Turkey and other countries. Where we in the UK may do with a bit of a punch up and kick in! These guys will use knives with no compulsion. If you feel you may get involved in trouble in foreign countries you would do well to check out the violent culture of the gangs and thugs before you go!

In Japan the act of violent crime is nearly non-existent. That's why you see Japanese tourist walking around London with 4 Nixon cameras worth a few grand around their necks without a care in the world. Or lending one to a total stranger to take a photograph of them. Their expectance of being mugged is nil because that's how they're conditioned. It's a dangerous frame of mind to be in, especially in a strange country.

I believe also self protection skills will vary depending on your environment. I have found people that train in Martial Arts within inner cities always have a very practical slant on what they do. Their techniques and emphasis are on the combat side of thing which is different to practising Martial Arts in the leafy suburbs!

If you live in an area where the potential of violent crime is high then you will certainly want to look after yourself. If you live in the country in a small quiet village your life is not centred around the dangers of violence. I have been asked why I still keep the emphasis on practical combat when I teach Martial Arts. Well until recently I lived in a multi cultural neighbourhood on one of the less selected sides of town all my life. It certainly isn't a war zone but it has it's fair of violent crime. The police helicopter regularly likes to scout the area. I was held up by knife point the other night and I could tell he was a local lad because he still had butter on the end of the blade! (Just joking). People that come to me for lessons are mostly in that 16 to 25 year old bracket that are obviously wary of going into a city centre on a Saturday night and they want techniques that have a practical edge if it gets physical.

So I am honest and try to teach them how it is, not to complicated, exotic and totally unpractical techniques.

I would love to tell them don't bother going into the city centre on a weekend, but obviously that won't happen. At that age it is almost complusory to go there, it's their social outlet. I will always teach avoidance first but obviously there are times when this isn't an option. There will be occasions where you will have to put up a hard front even if you are shaking like a leaf inside. You must learn to wear the 'game face'.

Some people will say, but I can't do that, it's not in my nature, I am not naturally aggressive. Here you must remember it's all an act. If I chose to be ultra aggressive, it is a ploy, inside I will still be in control, ice not fire.

Look at a film actor that you have seen in numerous films being the bad guy'. You then see him playing the lead in a romantic comedy and you are absolutely amazed that it's the same person. You have convinced yourself that he is a 'bad guy', this is down to great role play acting. You can do the same with practise. It's got to be good enough to plant a seed of doubt or unease in your antagonist, they are not sure of you should they push the situation? I have seen many people diffuse a potentially violent encounter with this method, even though I knew behind that front they were not particularly fighters. Where ignorance is bliss, confidence is king. There will be times to choose this solution, so make sure you are convincing in your own aggressive act and be prepared to back it up if you have to do so

Most aggressive situations are all hot air and words. Many don't escalate to much else. But prepare for abuse, shouting and cursing and still function without becoming engaged in what they are actually saying. It is pointless trying to analysis dialogue such as, 'You looking at me?', or 'What are you looking at?' Remember these are the street thugs entry techniques to see how you will react. If they detect fear they will hone in like a shark on blood. Be prepared for this kind of dialogue and have simple replys ready. If your reply to the question 'You looking at me? Is, 'Yes I am you ugly bastard' you will always be fighting. If it's instead a firm 'Sorry mate I thought I knew you from somewhere' It will probably blow over. It's all back to that ego again. It really controls which way you will go and the end result.

'A true warrior is a man who has the strength to walk away from a fight'!

Chapter 13
The Pack Mentality (Crowd violence/gang muggings)

There can be no more a frightening situation than being caught up in a large crowd that is starting to turn aggressive and violent. It is like being swept along in the wild river rapids without a canoe. You just have to go with the flow and hope you get out in one piece.

In the early and mid 70's 1 was an avid football supporter and enjoyed supporting my home team Bristol Rovers. Back then Rovers although a 3rd Division and 2nd Division outfit had many a good cup run that attracted many of the big 'then' first division clubs to their former Eastville stadium. Manchester United (with Best, Law, Charlton), Liverpool (with Keegan and Toshack) Stoke City (with Gordon Banks), Chelsea (with Osgood, Harris) and many more came to Bristol. So unfortunately did the mass crowd violence that seemed to be the hallmark of British football at that time.

Initially as a youngster I went to the matches with my Dad. I was glad of his protective arm around me at the end of the game, when we tried to get out of the ground and home before trouble flared. As a kid it was a frightening experience. I witnessed some pretty bad violence between supporters and also the police. Also I saw many an innocent fan hurt by mass crowd fighting. Later as a teenager I realised that I could also be a target for the violence and after a few close scapes I finally stopped going to the games for a long period of time.

Remember then it was standing on the terraces and when trouble started you were just pushed and shoved with the mass swell of bodies, if you fell under foot you were liable to be crushed to death or if you were squeezed up against crash barriers or the front pitch terracing. My Dad was always switched on and could see trouble developing and made sure we were most of the time in a reasonably safe place. There were though occasions when it didn't matter where you were standing you got caught up in it.

I liken impending crowd violence to a giant tidal wave building up at sea. First you experience a few ripples, then a couple of minor waves, then all of a sudden the big one comes! it can be overwhelming and extremely frightening.

Crowd violence has a 'domino effect'. It's a knock on syndrome just like a row of dominos. When one goes, they all go!

If you study video clips of football violence, protest marches, mob anarchy you will see groups moving in clusters together. They will explode with violent fighting, retreat, re-group and explode again. The crowd follows the lead of a few front runners and then it's the pack mentality taking over. People lashing out indiscriminately, punching, kicking, falling over, getting up, swinging wildly, throwing projectiles, using anything as a weapon etc. etc.

You can get caught up in this type of thing and be battered for no other reason than you are in the wrong place at the wrong time. If riot police arrive to break up the trouble don't expect them to ask questions first, they will wade in and hit anything that moves.

Crowd violence or multiple attacks on others can end up with tragic results. Gangs fuelled by alcohol or drugs can literally kick somebody to death, they have no conception of what they are doing. Kicking and stomping on people's heads will result in brain damage and death, yet thugs do this all the time. Why do some individuals survive a brutal 'kicking' like this? Purely luck and thats it. It only takes a kick to the head to be a quarter of an inch one way or the other to result in extreme injury. Sometimes the thread between life and death can be a very thin one.

In mass violence it doesn't matter how proficient you may be at defending yourself. In these circumstances anybody is fair game. I laugh sometimes at some Martial Arts displays of defending against multiple opponents. In reality there will be no blocking and countering of beautifully choreographed punches and kicks. Most will attack like a pack of wolves, in unison. You will be struck from all angles and pulled to the ground and kicked and stomped. If anybody thinks different they probably still believe in Father Christmas, the Tooth Fairy and that WWF wrestling is real!!!

Blood lust takes over here and people just go beserk. They have an extreme moment of madness fuelled by rage, frustration and primitive gut violence. Some will not even recall what they have done the next day. Throughout history there have been numerous cases of mob violence, lynch parties and revolts and rebellions. The violence was terrible. What about some of the crowd violence in Northern Ireland, the Middle East or some of the African countries? People have been shot, stabbed, butchered, hacked to death, strung up, burnt, dismembered, raped, tortured and God knows what else. As I said before the capacity for violence in a human being is huge.

We have perpetrated atrocities, disgusting and un-excusible things to other fellow humans.

Sometimes it doesn't always have to be violence that can make crowds dangerous. Panic is another if you are caught up in a scare with a fire alert or bomb scare. It only takes a few hysterical people to start a mass stampede with tragic results.

People can be strange creatures. In the January sales they will think nothing of pushing, stepping over, crushing and actually going hand to hand fighting with others over a sale item, something as minor as a pair of shoes or a shirt. It's practically kill or be killed! I avoid these sales like the plague, I don't wish to be man handled by hundreds of hysterical women (hey, hang on a minute, maybe that's not a bad thing?) No, reality check here most of them are like Nora Batty on acid. Joking aside, people have fainted, being trampled, battered and abused by the same people that were wishing them a happy New Year the night before!

When the petrol crisis was on here in the UK I witnessed the pure greed, ignorance, selfishness and blood lust of people clambering for their turn at the pumps. Blocking roads, swearing, cursing, abusing, pushing, shoving, fighting all to get first in the cue. The panic was widespread and totally over the top. Thank goodness Russia hadn't declared war on us, who knows what would have happened!

Crowds can be immensely claustrophobic and some people do get very panicy in them. When I was in the USA, my family and me went at the height of the holiday season some places were absolutely heaving. We visited places like Universal Studios and Disneyland and the crowds were immense, the queing phenomenal and you can see why people get edgy and also aggressive. It's a great experience to practise your self control techniques and aggression therapy. People will try any ploy to cue jump or get ahead. Some can be quite blatant. I can remember queing once in London with my wife and children to go into Madame Tussards. The waiting time was over two hours. My kids were great, seeing we had to stand all this time with it constantly drizzling. As we saw daylight at the front of the que, two Iranian guys pushed in front of us and another family claiming they had been in this spot in the cue and had just popped off to use a toilet. 1 know for a fact this was a lie and a blatant one. The other family didn't know what to say, as these guys were quite intimidating. I know I was going to have to step in so I let them know firmly that there was no way they were getting in this space.

They stood there looking at me, jabbering in their native tongue but I wasnt having any of it and they eventually backed off. It could have been a potentially dangerous situation, but I was pleased how I had handled it without dragging them out of the que by the scruff of their necks! My negotiating skills were vastly improving and it stopped the day from being spoiled.

Also in these large group events pick pockets are rife. You will be warned about this but so many ignore the fact. These people have handbags open, wallets in back pockets and are wondering around like lost sheep. It wont take long for a pick pocket to hone in on them.

In foreign countries this awareness has to be taken to an even higher level. My brother-in-law is a great traveller and has been to most places in the world and some decidedly 'dodgey' ones. He was informed by travel guides how pick pockets and thieves operate in different parts of the world and was told to abide by the rules or expect to lose his valuables.

Again in the States in certain areas your awareness had to be a 100%. In San Francisco which by the way is a beautiful city it also houses some of America's greatest collection of weirdos, pan-handlers, beggars and unstable citizens. When I visited I was at times on red alert and all my self protection scanning skills were put to great use. When we visited Alcatraz prison and they told us it was no longer in use I could have thought of a hundred odd people I had 'enjoyed in the city on the Bay' to fill it!

If you follow safe guidelines, keep switched on and abide by the rules in most crowds you will be fine, it's only when somebody neglects one of the above three rules that things can go wrong.

Whilst on the subject of crowds, we could also mention a lot of muggers or street thugs will work in small groups or couples. They will use this show of strength to demand what they want. A lone mugger knows that on his own he might not be able to pursuade a person to part with their valuables. Couples or gangs lend weight to the arguement.

I covered in some detail in my book 'In your Face' how to deal with multiple opponents. Here I just want to bring to your attention how they can work and operate. Gang muggings evolve around numbers closing in whilst one normally does the talking. It's this, corner the prey mentality. The threats can get overwhelming along with jostling and pushing. Victory and safety in numbers. Although they will work as a unit, there will always be a leader and instigator.

Couples work in many different ways. Again we can have the direct approach of two persons simply facing you off and intimidating you. One or both can bombard you with dialogue and keep you on the defensive. Another method is the disarming approach. Normally this can be worked by a male and female. The female may approach asking for directions or assistance. When you are engaged in conversatioon the male will demand your valuables. Alternative method is for one person to approach and engage you and then another to appear at your blind side and initiate an assault. This method is like another scene from Jurassic Park, when the hunter was engaged by the presence of a velocoraptor in front of him when it's mate attacked from the side. This he had been informed earlier was their prefered method of attack, but had been 'suckered' into the situation.

Weapons will normally be used as barganing tool to up the 'anti', in some cases threatening with syringes filled with so said 'Aids' infested blood. You must remember though that normally these will not be used if you comply, otherwise they would have used them at the start and taken what they wanted anyway.

Muggers have thought up many ingenious schemes to get what they want, A good friend of mine was held up and had his car keys taken off him and then he was 'charged' £50.00 to get them back!

In todays society we tend to be approached by many people when out on the streets some genuine, others not. Homeless begging for money, charity, collectors, sellers etc. As I mentioned, many are authentic, others have far more sinister purposes. The skill is to determine whose who. In my experience if you don't want to stop then don't, even if it might offend. Remember you are not obliged to help anybody and do be careful if you do. Of course there are time when you have to trust people but also trust your survival instincts because sometimes things aren't always as they seem. Here's another true tale of an ingenious scam.

A lady was driving along the road when she saw a baby wrapped in blankets in the gutter. She immediately pulled over and got out and went over to the child. On closer inspection she found out it was a child's doll. She went back to her car and carried on driving. Straight away she noticed a man in the car behind her flashing his lights, gesturing and driving very close to her bumper. She became uneasy and speeded up. Still the man pursued frantically signalling. Eventually she had to stop at traffic lights and saw the man get out of his car and run to her drivers side door . She was scared and clung to the handle. Just then she heard a noise behind her and saw a youth quickly scuttle from her back seat and out the door and run away,

When she had stopped abruptly to see the 'baby', the youth who planted it there jumped into the back seat. The man in the car behind had seen this happen and had followed the girl to warn her. As I said desperate people go to desperate measure!

My good friend Matthew Atkins who is a solicitor who has dealt with many violent crimes has always been a constant source of information to me on the different and varying modes of attacks on the street. Mugging always seems to follow a pattern.

This following description is actually from case notes from an old case of robbery that Matthew dealt with. Look at the scenario and see how it fits in perfectly with what I have been outlining. Robbery - June 97 Interview record.

'When the car stopped behind my moped I was standing beside my bike. A girl got out holding a piece of white paper in her hand. She asked me if I could tell her where a particular road was. Before I could see all the paper or answer, she pushed past me and grabbed my handbag from the box on the back of my moped. In an attempt to stop the girl I grabbed the bag and we struggled. Suddenly she produced a knife in her right hand. I cannot say where it came from and cut the straps of my bag. In seeing this I stepped back in shock and the girl then ran back to the car. Got in the passenger seat and the car sped off ....

I have read numerous cases with similar scenarios and it all goes back to you keeping safe distance and being wary. Yes it's hard to do, some muggers are very clever and devious but the only way to combat them is to stay switched on.

This chapter has explored the theory and techniques of crowd and multiple opponent violence. Please do absorb what has been written. It all comes from first hand experience. Mine or others. It is worth taking heed and being safe.

'The wolf rarely hunts alone, it will work in a pack'

Chapter 14
'Self Defence or Self Destruction'

'Learning to develop a knockout punch is 5% of a I00% self defence programme'

'Real Self Defence', Combat Orientated Systems, 'Street Protection', 'Realistic Defence Training': All these phrases and others alike have been spoken or written about in the Martial Arts circles in the last couple of years. In fact I feel now that most people are getting the message and probably beginning to tire of hearing these words bandied around.

Instructors like, Geoff Thompson, Peter Consterdine, Jamie O'Keefe, Dave Briggs, Dave Turton, Alan Charlton and others (myself included) have probably written about and covered every angle, topic, theory and tactic concerning Self Defence/Protection!

So what am I about to tell you on this well-worn subject that you haven't already heard? Hopefully some 'food for thought' on a few aspects that may have been overlooked or simply forgotten in this age of 'Realistic Training'. Bear with me and see what you think.

Today the line of thought is that if you haven't indulged in a I00 street fights then you can't be teaching Self Defence. Let me ask this question. Has a person involved in 100 street fights been practising sound self defence? If so, why is he always fighting?

Self Defence is not about fighting, in fact very little of it has to do with 'fighting'. Sure, you will have to deal with the issue of physical response but it won't be a fight, not if you get all the other factors right.

If any of you readers are familiar with the British Combat Association, you will know they developed something called the 'Protection Pyramid'. This pyramid includes all the aspects needed for a good self protection/ defence plan. Right at the top of the pyramid, the most narrow part of it, are the sections ranges/tools and targets. Basically this is the physical. Below this right down to the wide solid base are sections like personal security, threat awareness, evaluation and avoidance, fear control, attack scenarios and much more.

The physical response is the smallest part of the whole pyramid. A lot of 'so called' self defence experts are teaching only physical and nothing else. They are in that case teaching 'fighting techniques' not self defence.

Fighting techniques can range from grappling on the floor for sport, competition or a street fight to boxing, thai kicking/knees/elbows and so on. Fighting techniques for the ring, octagon etc have very little to do with self defence.

Good self defence is about avoidance and not being there when 'trouble kicks off'. It's about not being a victim. It's about understanding the street predators their actions, their talk and not falling prey to them, rather than punching, butting, biting and eye gouging.

Now those who know me or have read my books or articles may think I am contradicting myself, but let me explain.

I will not hesitate to use the above mentioned techniques and more if my life is in danger or if I have to defend my loved ones. I teach in my classes a whole host of brutal combat techniques. I can show you how to get a knockout blow in quickly or put a 'sleeper' strangle on, no problem, but I will also go to great lengths to explain that in a self defence situation this is my last resort. If I can't avoid or verbally diffuse a potentially dangerous situation and I am 'backed into a corner', then I will resort to physical technique and it will be something fast and final. I am a great believer in avoiding violence. I have had to deal physically with a lot less situations in the street compared to the literally dozens and dozens of times I have avoided or 'talked down' an impending violent encounter. I do pride myself on that fact more so than being able to recount to you the tales of battering hundreds of people. I believe I have got the practise of self defence right and I can pass useful information on to others.

I feel a lot of people, particularly some younger people in the martial arts at present, have the idea self defence is all about 'fighting' - If somebody gets in your face tell them to 'F*** off' batter them and complete the 'dance of death' on their prone bodies!

It is down to instructors, especially those who have a high profile in Martial Arts circles, who are teaching self defence to teach the younger and impressionable the right way. After all, students view their instructor as a figure head and will hang on their every word and actions

What you, as an instructor, say and teach will be taken as 'gospel' so you must get it right, otherwise you will only be developing predators like the ones you are supposedly teaching them to look out for! Then on a Saturday night in 'town' they will encounter their own 'mirror image' and a violent situation is bound to occur.

Think about that for a moment. I have met and encountered people like it! The martial arts world is notorious for them. You know them, they swagger on the mat, spitting and snarling, glaring at anybody who catches their eye. Arms splayed, chest puffed out, intent on letting you know how 'hard' they are. Me I couldn't give a damn how hard they are, I've seen it all before and I'm too long in the tooth now.

The men I really rate, the top draw martial artists don't have to wear their ego on their sleeves'. They have humility and respect about them and when they are 'not doing their thing', they are regular and approachable people. They have nothing to prove, the men I really admire and respect.

Self defence, self protection or as I like to think of it self preservation is a complete programme of training and totally different to standard martial arts classes, sparring sessions, training for competitions or no holds barred events. Those things are all about 'fighting techniques'. Great training, great fun and things I like to also spend time working on but they are not self defence training, bar some of the physical techniques that can be adapted for the street.

If a person came to a self defence class of mine and told me they had been the victim of constant muggings or violence I would primarily work on getting them to analyse why, change their habits, up their street awareness, teach evaluation and avoidance - all before I would teach them how to 'escape a stranglehold'. Why? Because otherwise they would be still fighting all their lives, they will still be a potential mugging or rape victim and I will only have addressed the immediate 'illness', not prescribed a long term cure! That is real self defence, it's a way of life not a few fancy tricks.

Society is aggressive enough, wherever you go there is some form of it. Physical self defence techniques are most certainly needed and do have to be employed when you have exhausted all other options. Employing 'physical' because someone is eyeing up your girlfriend, has spilt your beer, supports a different football team, or is a different race, colour or creed is not self defence, it's fighting for the sake of fighting. Because somewhere along the way somebody has programmed your brain to react in that way. Some influence or peer pressure has sold you some macho crap that you have swallowed hook, line and sinker and you believe it, you believe your motives and methods are right. Fighting is fighting whether it's on the 'cobbles', or in the ring, or on the mats. Everybody involved in martial arts wants to develop the best fighting technique and quite rightly so. When you have achieved this, knowing when to use these techniques appropriately is of prime importance if you get it wrong you may be clashing with your friendly neighbourhood constabulary once too often and may find yourself a guest at one of HMS hotels! (you know - the ones where they throw away the key!)

Everybody at present seems to want to prove their fighting abilities in one shape or form. Well, there are many avenues to explore to do this. Try one of the freestyle grappling competitions that are around, or go for ML Sports MMA Combat Trials or Tudo format, get in a boxing ring, or try Geoff Thompson' Animal Day sessions, this is where the fighting is done.

Self defence skills are a whole different 'ball game' where you are training for a completely different situation. Understanding the difference is important. Teaching the difference is also important, don't get it confused with anything else.

Why do I mention all these points? Because until I learnt different somewhere along the line in my 30 years of martial arts training, I have made most of the mistakes I have mentioned in this article! But I am big enough to hold my hands up and admit it. Are you?

'More than an end to war, we want an end to the beginnings of all wars' Franklin D Roosevelt

Chapter 15
'Cerebral Defence

Throughout this book we have explored the behavioural habits of the aggressive and violent person and we have learnt that to deal with these people we first and foremost must work using our heads. We use react with our minds not our emotions. The saying 'fools rush in where angels fear to tread', is a good one when it comes down to dealing with a dangerous situation.

How would you act under the pressure of violent confrontation? Maybe you know or maybe you don't. If you don't, think back to how you reacted in some sort of crisis in your life. Did you take control of the issue and attempt to deal with it in a controlled manner or did you run around like a headless chicken in a panic? This should give you an answer to your character and how you would react.

Taking a moment to sum up a situation is vital if you want to get this right. For example if a work colleague comes up to you and said that the guy working in the front office reckoned you were a waste of space and a w ---- r, how would you deal with it? Would you rush straight into the office for a confrontation, spitting and swearing abuse or would you take time out and ask your work colleague did they hear this from the person themselves, or was this second hand information? Very often people will get the wrong end of the stick or exaggerate a situation, so that you go in all guns blazing and make a fool out of yourself.

I can relate to this in my younger days. I would get a snippet of information at work that I didn't agree with and go hammering on the manager's door to confront them in an aggressive mood. I have had toe to toe arguments, intimidating and threatening arguments, pushing, shoving arguments and worse. My temper at that time was definitely on a knife edge and I wasn't open to much in the way of reasoning. You see I hate people taking advantage of their positions and taking liberties it's just another form of bullying which I also detest.

I found though sometimes I got myself into bigger trouble by my approach and had to learn to be more tolerant.

In my Martial Arts training I had become the same. I had a reputation for being very hard when I practised. Again I admit at one stage I became the bully that I despised but I couldn't stop it, I enjoyed having that power. I know certain people did not want to train with me but that made it all the better when I caught up with them. Compromise was not in my criteria and I treated everybody the same. If I met somebody that fancied themselves as a bit handy I had to go out of my way to prove that they weren't.

I travelled all over the UK on seminars training and left a mark where ever I went. In my 20's I was extremely aggressive on the mats and I hurt many people, some who didn't deserve it. I could fill a book with stories, but this is not the place. Enough to say I have mellowed somewhat from those days! I realised as I started to think more about situations I could see other solutions and means to solve a problem. Many, under pressure, react before they think and then live to regret it. I feel we should always have a scheme up our sleeves to deal with different aggressive or violent scenarios. If you do this, you will have a 'battle plan' to work by.

Take this scenario as an example of taking just a few seconds to think how you need to play it.

You wake up in the early hours of the morning and hear a noise outside.

You look out of your bedroom window and see three youths around your car up to no good. In your anger and shock you run down stairs and out the front door to confront them. You yell out 'What the hell are you doing?' these guys turn around with no fear or surprise on their faces and confront you. You notice two of them have knives. How intimidating are you stood bare footed in nothing but your 'boxers', empty handed and above all empty headed. AS the youths approach you, you momentarily wonder if plucking a handful of 'daffs' from the front garden and throwing them at the advancing trio will help! You decide not and turn to run back to the sanctuary of your house. That's when you noticed the front door has slammed shut with the wind! Not the best of strageties. A rush of blood to the head and now you find yourself in a worse position.

Let's rerun this scenario again. Whilst looking out of the bedroom window, open it and shout from there, *'Get away from that car or I'll call the police!'* That should do the trick. If the group laugh and tell you where to go, then you have to decide if you wish to confront them, if you do make that decision, get some trousers and shoes on at least and then get an 'equaliser' in the way of a weapon. Something big, visual and frightening that gives the outright message 'this hurts'. A baseball bat, samurai sword, or something along the same lines. This time when you confront them let them know they are going to get one last warning and be demonstrative with the weapon so it leaves them in no doubt that they have picked the wrong person. Even if inside you don't intend to use the weapon at least your overall visual appearance looks better than you stood in your boxer shorts with a handful of daffodils!

Always give warning first and give a person(s) a chance to run or back off. If they mock this warning and get more aggressive and abusive you will have to go to plan B and get 'tough'. It must be convincing and you must be prepared to bring them right up to the cliff edge of violence and if necessary and finally give them a push.

As always try to de-escalate and give them a loophole for escape but if they don't take this route you will have to change tact.

I have found myself in many a situation that has made me feel very uncomfortable. I have maybe been in a bus que or actually riding public transport with my family when a group of youths are sharing the same space and are continually using foul language in the presence of my then young children. In these situations I feel the bubbling feeling of adrenalin in the pit of my stomach and I hate the feeling every time it occurs. I just know that there is going to be confrontation.

Now if I had an opportunity to leave the facinity then I would be saving my family or myself any grief, sometimes though you can't and you just know that you are going to have to do something about the situation.

I have learnt over the years from experience to pre-plan your move do not act on emotion. Know actually what you are going to say and be prepared for a retort or a 'woof' as American Self Defence expert 'Marc Mac Young' might say. This means some sarcastic put down or come on when somebody doesn't rate your seriousness.

When you decide to confront a problem like the one I have described here. Be polite but firm, show no fear or have no quaver in your voice. Give them that option to apologize or back down.

In these situations I have said 'Hey lads do you mind cutting out the language I've got young children here?' Then I see how it goes and play it from there. I have been faced with different replies like, 'Sorry mate ok' Stunned silence, Looks of wounded pride, and most annoyingly stupid smirks and the odd individual saying 'It wasn't me'. (There's a song in there somewhere!)

If I get anymore grief I will separate the 'main man' from the pack and have a little word with him and see if I can in a pretty simple manner persuade him it's not in his best interests to carry on the way him and his cronies are. You see I don't want all the hassle that comes with a physical situation. Police, courts, hospitals, emotional trauma. I want to enjoy my life and avoid societies morons. I am not afraid of physical, I know I can handle it, but the more I learn the less inclined I am to use it. I have learnt this over a long period of time and I go on learning everyday. To control natural aggression is a hard task and one that constantly needs monitoring.

I have a destinct view of what I feel is right and wrong. I hate bullying, people taking advantage or liberties and treating others like dirt. I know I will react to these things but know I do it in a controlled manner and not just fly off the handle.

I have found the above scenarios much more of a trial than any physical encounter. When a situation goes physical you just do what you do, win or lose, you don't really have time to think you just react.

In instances of impending trouble you can have internal battles in your mind on how you will deal with it. You have to beat off negative thoughts before you can get positive ones. I truly hate these scenarios, they are very uncomfortable.

I can remember a story told to me by one of my ex-Martial Arts students. This guy was a lovely man, not a fighter but somebody who came to me to increase his confidence and actually became a very promising Martial Artist. He told me this tale about 6 months after he started training with me. He was in a restaurant with his girlfriend, sitting at a table ready to enjoy a special meal together. At the bar were 3 or 4 drunken men, being foul mouthed and lets say a little 'laddish'. My friend said he was aware of them and he got very uncomfortable about the bad language in front of his lady. He said he tried to ignore it but it got worse and he knew he was going to have to do something. He related, I sat down and thought of the outcome of me approaching these guys and I saw it was probably going to get physical and I would take a beating, but I couldn't let this situation go on and spoil the evening. As I got up and approached them my legs felt like jelly and I almost bottled it but I kept going and addressed them. Excuse me guys, could you do me a favour and keep the language down, I'm with my girlfriend over here?' He waited for the first punch to swing. But no, instead they apologized, they didn't realise and they had had one too many. They moved off with no hassle to another part of the room.

My friend said when he turned around to walk back to his table he felt about ten foot tall and he couldn't help put a small swagger into his step! He had handled a potentially dangerous situation with skill and it had worked. He told me without the confidence he had gained through my classes he would never have approached these guys in the first place. I was pleased for him.

Rational thought will always beat 'hot headedness'. Controlled aggression better than untamed aggression. Channel it correctly and you are on to a winner.

The best military leaders in history were not only extremely good fighters but were brilliant strategists with sharp and clever brains. They never just waded into battle without forethought and plan, otherwise-death count and casualty list of their own men would have been extreme. They used their skills of strategic warfare to the maximum before actually having to engage in any physical assault.

The Greeks, Romans, Vikings and Mongols all had great leaders who were brilliant planners as well as ferocious warriors. The feared Mongol leader Genghis Khan was known as an invincible warrior but he also was an extremely clever man. That's why he achieved the things he did and booked his place in history along with others like Oliver Cromwell, Napoleon, Nelson, Peter the Great and many more. We must try and be the same " think before we act otherwise the act can be costly. It's not a matter Sometimes if whether you can physically beat somebody or not. It may in the circumstances be more prudent to beat a retreat. For instance with the incidents with the youths I mentioned earlier on. I could of quite easily waded in and started taking them out, but the consequences could have been a lengthy prison term for me. If God forbid I ever have to 'do so' I want to think it would have to be a life threatening situation to bring me to that conclusion not some stupid and pointless arguement. Many are 'inside' now for much less, fortified by a moment of madness.

'It's possible to disagree with someone about the ethics of non-violence without wanting to kick his face in' quote.

Chapter I6
Survival steps to dealing with violent people

'Walk softly and carry a big stick - President Roosevelt

Somewhere when life is going well for you and you are enjoying yourself you are certain to meet an a--h--e! It's the law of averages, simply because there are so many of them around.

You may meet an aggressive person during the course of your employment and you may have a position at your job that requires you to deal with them. You must be prepared for this and have some plan already worked out on how you are going to deal with such a person.

If this person is a disgruntled employee or customer then hopefully you will be able to talk them down into a more reasonable frame of mind. Separate them from any audience and get them to sit down, this is always a good start. Don't hide behind company policy, technical jargon. Do not talk down to them and use your authority to belittle or humiliate. Be sympathetic but also firm. Show concern and do listen to what the person is saying otherwise this will only inflame the situation. If they are cursing and swearing then tell them you will not carry on the conversation if they keep up the abuse .

Find out the real cause of their problem quickly and try to resolve it. Put the ball in their court and ask them what they think you should do, this gets them to think rationally and positively, rather than ranting and raving.

If the situation gets out of hand and you feel intimidated, find an excuse to leave the office and go for help or back up. Make sure you are never cornered and have easy excess to leave. Closing an office door can produce an air of privacy but can also cut you off from any outside help. If you have to discipline an employee always have a witness there to give support and monitor the situation. Never do these things alone. Some people will react to discipline in an aggressive way and it may well become physical. Carry this carefully and safely.

There are many principles for dealing with work place violence. 'Streetwise' by Peter Consterdine, which is an excellent book, devotes chapters to this subject and is well worth checking out.

In my opinion Peter is the premier self protection consultant in the Uk. I personally run 'safe and sound' conflict management seminars for anybody interested in this particular line of training.

If we up the scale and have to confront an extremely hostile person you must again have a game plan. Once again do not patronise or talk down to them. Do not touch them as this may trigger off violence or they may claim you assaulted them. Do not turn your back on this type of person for one minute even if you think you have the situation under control. These individuals can be dangerous and unpredictable. I have seen many a person apoligize and look to shake hands with another and then strike them unexpectedly.

On this note also don't surprise a person who may react violently. For example if you come across somebody breaking into your car, shout out a warning at distance first. This will give them time to run and leave your car. OK they get away but at least your property and more importantly you are in one piece!

If you choose to sneak up behind them and shout 'what the hell are you doing?' The shock may force them to panic, turn and lash out. Many have been stabbed using this strategy. Remember if you corner a frightened animal they will fight back because they have no choice. If they have a gap to get away they will choose this, so be careful with your approach.

Many years ago, as foreman of a timer yard I was called and told somebody was in our car park looking into the open back of a customers van. I was first to go out to the car park and saw a young guy bent over rummaging in this van. I knew the builder had an assortment of tools in there that could be used in panic as a weapon, so I kept my distance and called out, 'What are you doing?' The guy abruptly turned around and stared at me. I told him to get away from the van. He began to walk towards me. I immediately switched on and shifted my body into a small 45% stance and put up my invisible guard with my hands to protect my space. As he got closer I knew he was on some type of substance. His eyes were totally glazed and lifeless. He mouthed words but nothing was coherent. I told him to leave. He stood there swaying slightly and I though for one second he was going to try an attack. Just then the builder whose van it was and a few other guys arrived and the youth stumbled off. I knew if I had ran out to him without thought and grabbed him it may well of escalated into something nasty. I'm sure I could have handled that but why take the risk. Nothing was taken from the van and no harm done. Good result.

In that job over the years I met and encountered many aggressive and in some cases unstable people and handled most of them correctly. But I learnt you had to really be switched on and try many different approaches to resolving the situation but I never ever used the little authority I had to intimidate others. People's anger can surface in many different ways and you need to understand this. Please read Jamie O'Keefe's superb book 'No one fears when angry'. This text turns this subject inside out, all done in Jamie's 'no holds barred' way! A must read for anybody who wants to find out the many facets of anger.

When you approach a potentially violent person scan their hands for weapons. If a hand is hidden presume they are 'carrying'. Keep your distance and spread your hands in an open non-aggressive manner. Talk to them try and diffuse the situation. Let your voice and body language mirror each other. It is no good telling a person you don't want any trouble while coiled in your karate kid stance!

Keep scanning, watch their eyes, do not get caught up with their threats or abuse. If they scream 'don't come any closer, don't touch me!' Then reply 'Hey ok I'm staying here, now take it easy or put the weapon down, the police are on their way, don't make things worse for yourself'. Be firm, but calm. Show that you are in charge and put forward the impression you have done this loads of times before even if it is the first time. Remember the acting. If you can convince them they will fall for it.

All the time be prepared if they come at you to strike them pre-emptively, hard and fast. You must do this to protect yourself and it will be justified if you felt you were in danger. (Ref.'The Fence', Geoff Thompson: Pre-emptive strikes for winning fights' - Jamie O'Keefe).

We would all like to diffuse violence without resorting to greater violence but I live in the real world and know some people will not let you do this and will push you through that doorway to physical response.

I will always give people a loophole to walk away from violence, this will be my first response. If I am in the wrong I am big enough to acknowledge this and apoligize. But if I am cornered and have no choice I will strike and strike first, I will not be bullied, or endure bullying. 'A cornered beast is a dangerous beast' 'Understand the difference between a dog's bark and a dog's growl!'

Chapter I7
'Time to Tame aggression'

Below I have listed some different scenarios for you the reader to study and then role play with a friend. The idea behind these simple tests are for you to use your verbal de-escalation skills to prevent a violent encounter. If you never practise these verbal skills you will not have them at your disposal when you need them most. For anybody involved in Martial Arts you need to practise these verbal scenarios as often as any punch or kick.

Remember physical violence has to be our last choice, verbal de-escalation one of the first.

Try these scenarios and try and develop dialogue to diffuse what could be a particularly dangerous situation.

1) You unknowingly drive into somebody else's parking space. As you get out of your car you are confronted by an extremely angry male in his 50's. He shouts at you, 'Owi, that's my f ----- g parking space what's your game?'

2) You are stood in a pub at the bar when you glance around and see a large aggressive looking individual staring at you. He seems to take offence to you looking and shouts 'What the f-k are you looking at?' He then strides across towards you.

3) You are stopped in the street by an individual who asks for directions to a certain place. As you begin to tell them he suddenly change tact and ask's for your wallet.

4) A work colleague comes to you with a gripe. You are busy and tell them to come back later. They suddenly explode into a torrent of verbal abuse and become very animated.

5) You are waiting in a que at an ice-cream van to get your kids an ice lolly when two youths que jump with a snigger and line up ahead of you.

6) A street vagrant pursues you for some change. You refuse and carry on walking. They follow you and become abusive and confrontational.

7) As a lone female you are struggling back to your car with some heavy shopping bags. Your car is in a multi story car park. As you near your vehicle a man approaches you and

offers to help. You are wary of him and politely refuse. He persists with the offer, although you have again said no. He then becomes irrate calling you a 'stuck up bitch.'

8) You come out of a hypermarket and head for your car, as you near your vehicle you see three youths hanging around it. One is sat on the bonnet. As you get nearer you ask them to get away from the car. They sneer at you and one says 'What are you going to do about it?'

9) You are sat in a crowded train with your wife and children. Across the aisle sits two drunk males who have become loud and are using foul language frequently, with no regard for those around them.

10)   Standing at a bus stop late evening, a rather strange individual approaches you, mattering and cursing under his breath. He stands at the bus stop and tries to engage you in his crazy conversation.

The ten are all common ones, that you could encounter any time Most of them I have experienced and didn't have to resort to violence in any of them., If your answer to each scenario is 'Punch their lights out,' you are on your way eventually for a spell at her majesty's pleasure. Even if you are fully capable of physically handling the situation, using verbal self defence must be your first option, always. If you feel at this moment that you may get tongued tied or dry up completely in these situations then start learning confrontation dialogue with a friend and take some verbal bullets on board to protect yourself.

We can all feel fear in some shape or form when confronted but this is only natural when we embark on the unknown strange or dangerous. Geoff Thompson' best selling book 'Fear, the friend of exceptional people' by Summerdale puts fear into perspective and will help you understand and control it.

When aggression comes along, it does shake the average person up because they are not used to it. People like the police, door security, supervisors, etc are exposed to aggression on a regular basis and are used to living with it, others arent and feel afraid, again this is natural. Read 'Fear' and you will be better prepared when violence rears it's ugly head and be able to still function under extreme stress. Remember F.E.A.R. means False Evidence Appearing Real.

Writer Sarah Utterbach says '*If you destroy the negative, the picture can never be developed. Fear is just a darkroom where all our negatives are developed. It'll intimidate you if you let it.*'

Do not fear going forward slowly. Fear only to stand still.

Chapter 18
'Armed and Dangerous'

As mentioned earlier in this book many cultures will use weapons as their first line of attack or defence. The knife is the weapon of choice in many - especially in Asia and the Far East. Fist fights are not the normal occurence, as here in the Western World. Their disputes are settled with blades. I remember a story my good friend and fellow Martial Artist, Paul Flett related to me on this subject.

In his younger days he was in the Merchant Navy and stopped off at many a port around the world. On a dock in the Philipinnes he witnessed two locals have a dispute which ended up as a fight. Both produced Balisong Butterfly knives (a notorious knife in this part of the world) and started slashing and stabbing at each other. A crowd gathered to see the spectacle. It wasn't anything out of the ordinary to them but it certainly at the time shocked Paul.

In African countries machetes and large bladed knives are used in fights, riots and other distrubances with regularity. South American countries also use the knife exclusively over$ any other weapon for fights and muggings.

In the 80's here in the UK knives became prominent in street fights and many people carried them. There were some horrific incidents on the streets and also in nightclubs. When the weapons amnesty came into force it seemed to reduce the use of this and other weapons in our society, which thankfully was a good thing.

America of course has a gun culture and in recent times some terrible and tragic incidents have occured with random and multiple killings using guns. Mass killings at high schools, fast food restaurants and shopping Malls have occured on more than one occasion and many innocent people lost their lives because of some deluded psychopath with a grudge.

But these incidents aren't just confined to the USA. Although thankfully only in their minority, our own Uk has suffered similiar incidents. The Hungerford massacre, the maniac with a machete in the school playground and the tragic death of the lovely Jill Dando, are among some of a handful of violent scenarios.

Each gang culture here in the UK had their weapons of choice. The Teddy boys had cut throat razors, bikers used heavy bike chains, Mods carried flick knives, the 'bootboys' of the soccer violent era preferred sharpened steel combs and so it goes on.

Weapons are prevailent in our societies and probably always will be. WE must be aware to this fact and watch out for them if involved in a violent alteration. Many stories are published in the newspapers about a person or persons confronting another only to be stabbed, blugeoned or shot. Some people no longer seem to care about the extent of injury they will inflict. Just look at the high profile cases of the needless and appalling murder of Steven Lawrence. I crimes of rape or sexual assault against women, a knife or similiar will be used by the attacker to control and empower their victim. Remember rape is a crime of power and control, not necessarily sex. The knife emphasises this power. The attacker will love to see the fear on their victim's face, it will only go to highten their excitement.

Muggers will also use a weapon to enforce their demands for your money or valuables. Remember they don't want a stand up fight they want to commit the crime and get away as soon as possible. The weapon gives them more control and the less chance of the victim fighting back.

As mentioned in my book 'In your face,' the only light at the end of the tunnel in these situations is that if the attacker wanted to use the weapon they would have done so straight off and taken your valuables or assaulted you after you were incapacitated with a stab wound.

They still may use the weapon but the likely hood of them using it is a small one. The tactics and techniques of handling these scenarios are covered fully in 'In your face'.

Knives are a very visual weapon and strike fear into most people that's why these street predators use them, plus it's a lot easier to obtain a knife then a firearm. Also if you choose to carry a firearm and use it, the consequences are usually fatal and if caught you will be looking at a long term prison sentence.

The knife has also been ingrained in our sub-conscious as the frightening weapon of a madman or killer. If we go back again to the film world and recall Psycho', Halloween, Friday the 13th, Scream and many other slasher movies we just know the helpless girl, the dumb boyfriend or the incredibly stupid gang of teenagers are going to be slaughtered! It again has become part of our mental programming and the fear is inbreed in us.

From the beginning of time man has looked for better and more powerful weapons. From flint knives and axes right through to high tech weaponary and nucleur weapons, man has a fascination for tools of destruction.

Amazingly our own police force for many years were inadequately armed, with the anarchic wooden truncheon. While criminals sported knives, revolvers, shotguns and like, the police were lagging well behind in this country compared to others. It took many a tragic death and continual complaints by the 'Bobbie on the beat', before the powers to be allowed the use of the ASP (extended steel baton) and CS gas spray to be issued to them. The fuss, red tape and debate that went on before this decision was made, was incredible. I know if I was a lone police officer confronted by a maniac waving a machete I would want every equaliser available to me! I see now the authorities are considering electrical stun guns and pepper spray to combat crime. Bloody good show, let's get on with it and quickly.

The Uk was worried about the image of our traditional Bobby and how it would effect them in relation to the public. Well I don't know about you but when I have been in a different country and I have seen a police officer with a side firearm and a bloody big baton strapped to his leg, I get the over whelming urge to call him 'sir'. Our police have taken enough shit from societies scum. If arming them in some way gains them respect again then I'm all for it.

'A weapon is only as dangerous as the man who uses it!' Quote.

Chapter 19
'The Dark Side'

'Well we all have a face that we hide away forever and we take them out and show ourselves when everyone has gone!'
- from the song 'The stranger' by Billy Joel

In this book we have examined the many guises of violence and aggression. A lot of it can be up front and 'In your Face', it's easy to see coming and it is not disguised in any way. But some people can be masters of disguise and can hide their 'dark side' very well until it's time to reveal it.

For example take the lady who finds her Prince Charming. A man who is courteous, charming and caring. A wonderful person and an ideal partner. They decide to live together or get married and then somewhere along the way the violent side of this 'ideal man' surfaces. Prince Charming has become the Beast!

Many woman have walked into violent relationships unknowingly and then paid the price. Some of these relationships have been celebrity and high profile status, but many many more go undetected, day in, day out. The men perpetrating the abuse can hide this side of his character very well. At work he may be well liked. Down the pub he's Jack the lad. Other women will find him attractive. Yet behind closed doors he becomes a monster that flys into a violent rage at little or no provocation.

In his latest book *'No-one fears when angry'*, my good friend Jamie O'Keefe writes in length about this subject and his total disgust for the wife beater or woman abuser and I am in complete agreement with him.

There can be no excuse for this behaviour. Any excuse is a sign of weakness. Alcohol, stress and many other reasons are put forward to explain the behaviour, but they are pathetic reasons. The problems go deeper than this and you will probably find this type of person has had these violent urges from a young age and got away with it, believing it was alright to abuse woman. Maybe their father abused their mother and so on, I don't know but to carry on in this fashion can only lead to disaster.

As mentioned earlier the rapist can also be a Mr. Charming and indeed many are, this is how they get close to their victims and then they suddenly change into their 'dark side'.

I feel the story of Mr. Jackal and Mr. Hyde was really telling us about mans nature to have a good and evil side and how maybe some individuals struggle to keep the balance.

Many rapists, serial killers and abusers have gone for long periods of time without committing any crime and then suddenly as if the evil side of them has caught control they start again.

We can all be guilty of being two faced on occasions. We can smile and speak to somebody, then as soon as they leave the room we will slag them off behind their backs! We all have another face that we always don't want people to see, but for most of the time there is not anything too sinister to this, others though can hide appalling secrets, for instance Fred West, the genial builder, known and liked by everyone, they didn't realise the terrible side of his nature he was hiding. As mentioned some people are masters of disguise. They can worm their way into your confidence or affection in a seemingly innocent way. They can go undetected for years and years.

It is a frightening thought that there could be serial killers wandering around in our society, unknown to us but they could be sat next to you on the bus. In the USA the FBI admit there are probably hundreds of serial killers roaming the country not yet detected or caught. A chilling thought.

We have to accept there are many dangerous and unstable people in our society and you may just be the person that runs into them. Acceptance of this fact is important. No one is immune or excluded from becoming a victim.

As I am writing this book I have read many cases of violence in the newspaper and it all seems to be getting worse. Everyday you can pick some incident of violence that has occured. We need to be ever vigilant and do our upmost to avoid the darkside of society.

Chapter 20
'Once there were warriors'

I re-watched the film 'Braveheart', the other evening on TV. Which portrayed the story of William Wallace and the Scottish fight for independence back in the rule of Edward the First. A friend of mine remarked the following day that these men must have had unbelievable courage and guts to go into battle the way they did and I agreed whole heartedly that they had, but also remarked that they had grown up knowing nothing else. They were born to be fighters, because their whole existence relied on this fact. My friend Jamie O'Keefe said that all we mostly fight against on a daily basis is 'traffic and sleep.'

We in todays society do not have to fight for land, property, food etc, the majority of us are lucky in this regard. Back then it was the done thing, so men were trained to fight on a daily basis as part of their routine of survival, they knew no different.

In our so called 'civilised' existence we do not have to face the fact that we will be fighting for our lives each day as we leave our houses for work, so our mind set is different to the mindset of those warriors of yesteryear.

Their expectancy and acceptance of facing violent or life threatening situations were high and they learned to deal with this and although they most certainly felt fear, they could overide the negative feelings it gave and replace them with the positive.

You may say that you couldn't do this, but if you are a father or a mother and you saw your child being hurt, abused, abducted, etc you would overide all fear for your own safety and do what you had to do to save them.

You see we all still have that warrior mentality deep down inside. It is one of our god given traits. It is our survival instincts and if trained correctly they can be 'tapped into' when needed. The problem for some is the feelings may have been dormant for years and they find it hard to unearth or even understand them. These individuals constantly live in fear of violence and believe they are powerless to do anything about it. This is not true, you can change and rid yourself of these negative feelings. I highly recommend you read Geoff Thompson's excellent book 'Fear, the Friend of exceptional people' to understand more on this subject.

There are others in our society that would definately been on those battlefields of old, banging their swords on their shields and chanting. These people have found productive outlets for their aggressive and competitive nature. Rugby players, Boxers, Martial Artists, Ice hockey players and many more are prime examples. Part of them live with those primeval feelings of the warriors of yesteryear and they thrive on the rush of adrenilin and fear, they have got to have this as part of their lives. Why do you think it's so hard for example for a boxer to retire. Some have all the money they could ever need, but it's the warrior instinct that keeps going, they need it, without this they don't feel right, they become restless.

The soldiers and warriors of days gone by were the same. When not in battle for long periods of time, they had to set up 'mock' fights to keep them sharp and entertained, for example the josting tournaments of the English knights. I believe the saying once a fighter, always a fighter. It will stay with you in some shape or form for life.

I recently was lucky enough to meet on a seminar Roy 'pretty boy' Shaw. Roy was a famous unlicensed boxer, a bare knuckle champ and an awesome street fighter as well, with a huge reputation. Roy is now in his 60's but he is still every inch a fighter. He no longer needs to fight and is a successful business man but part of him is and still will be a 'fighter'. It is inbreed in him and that won't change. There are many more like him.

Aggression and fighting spirit are not bad things, chanelled correctly they are fine attributes and one's that we do need. We may not be the warriors of days gone by, but we should never lose those basic instincts for survival when needed. We should look to train and develop these skills so if needed we can bring them to the surface more readily. OK for some of us we may not have the time or inclination to train to be a Martial Artist or Boxer but sometime spent studying the rules of self protection and the physical skills of a good self defence programme can prove invaluable. Self protection skills can then become a skill for life, no matter where you travel or what path your life will take you.

Just as most people would not dream of not having home insurance, life insurance, car insurance, travel insurance etc, think of self protection skills as another of those insurance polices. As we hope we may never have to claim for our house being burgled or being flooded, we also hope we never have to use our physical skills to fight off a violent attack. But isn't it sensible to have some pro-active plans for these eventualities incase they arrive? It amazes me that the average person has no real idea of how to defend themselves, or they have some ludicrous half baked idea of what works. Yet these same people could probably tell you how to stop a shark attack, avoid and escape a smoke filled building or survive a mountain avalache. The likelihood of these things happening compared to encountering a violent attack, mugging etc are minimal yet they put greater thought and energy into those scenarios than learning what to do is somebody grabs you around the neck whilst getting into your car! I think everybody should have some basic self protection skills taught to them. Schools for instance are supposed to be preparing our children for the 'real world' yet none teach self protection programmes, especially for young ladies. Colleges, the workplace, and all industries should have a good self protection programme in place, many don't.

The warriors through history were always prepared to defend home and livelihood, yet in this day and age the majority have not got a clue. They will live with the dangerous attitude of 'it can't happen to me', this is a very naive stance to take. An ounce of prevention is better than a pound of cure.

But what of the violent members of society, would they have been warriors of old? Yes probably, but they have no positive route to channel their aggressive tendencies. They would have been undisciplined and rogue warriors wanting to fight purely for fightings sake.

Today they are the face of football hooligans, rioters, wife beaters, killers and like. The aggression somewhere has been lost to uncontrollable blood lust, anger and hatred, against anything or anybody, they are lose cannons, some physopaths, with no conscience or remorse. Do you think these people are in the minority? Then stand outside a pub, nightclub or taxi rank on a Saturday night in any city centre and you will witness them in their droves. These peoples aggression and violence will spill uncontrollably over just to get infront in a taxi que. They will viciously batter somebody to a pulp to get there and take that taxi home without a backward glance. These individuals are not 'hard', they are bloody dangerous and unpredictable. Some in my opinion should not even be walking around free in our society. They are like the big cat that has become a man killer or the rogue dog that attacks indiscriminitally. When these creatures are captured they are put down, no questions asked! Enough said, I think!

Remember the warriors of yesteryear fought for survival, for life itself, they didn't fight or kill for pure pleasure, only the physcopath does this. Warriors had codes of honour, ethics and respect. These animals on the street today have none of those things and have no respect for their fellow man.

Look recently in the news at the so called Race Riots in Bradford, or the mass fighting and the one tragic death at 'peace' talks in Genoa. Whatever the demonstration this 'hardcore' element are there for one reason and one only .... Violence! The purpose of the demonstration means nothing to them, it is just a good excuse for anarchy and bloodshed. This is our modern society. When you see these things you have to wonder how far we have really come in becoming civilised? Modern technology of computers, internet and it's like doesn't hide the fact that man is still a destructive creature, who doesn't carry much respect of his own species.

Yes once there were warriors and many were called 'Barbarians, animals and savages' When you view some of the images of world violence flash across our TV screens, you can't help but wonder what some of the human race are now?

'We need more understanding of human nature because the only real danger that exists is man himself.' Carl Jung

Chapter 21
'It's only words'

Words are powerful weapons and can invoke many emotions when used against US.

Remember at the start of this book when I said how hurtful children can be with words to each other? From the day we see how people react to our words, is the day we learn all about the use of intimidation, threats, blackmail and other forms of verbal menace. Although in our young life it may all be in it's infancy, the fruits have been sown for later life.

If we take a trip back to childhood may be we can recall words that would conjure up feelings of dread. There's a few that I can personally recall:

'It's 7.30, time to get up for school!'

'Wait to your father gets home!'

It's double maths first lesson!'

'Time to get out of the shallow end of the pool young man and move up to the deep end!'

'Joe Bloggs is looking for you!'

'Time for bed, school tomorrow (Sunday evening)'

To some people these above statements may not bother them whatsoever, but for me as a 12 year old boy, it was next to the end of the world! You see a few words can either make or break your day. It's not so much the words themselves but it is the context that they are used in that matters It's like the old joke about the man having a bath when a knock sounded on the front door. The man shouted out 'What is it, I'm in the bath? A voice replied, *'I'm the man from Littlewoods.'* The guy in the bath thinks, Littlewoods, I must have won the football pools. He races downstairs and opens the door. Excitedly he says *'Yes, what is it?'* The man at the door replies, *'I'm sorry sir, but we have just caught your wife shoplifting!'* Right words wrong context, change the whole scenario.

Our minds can conjure up many horrific and frightening images when certain dialogue can be used against you. 'The boss wants to see you in his office now', can get people breaking out in a cold sweat, wondering what he/ she wants. On the trip to their office you will turn over every thing you have done the last few days, to figure out if you have done anything wrong. When you get to their office and they speak with you, you find out they are putting you forward for a rise in your salary. Suddenly the whole situation is turned on it's head.

There are other scenarios that spell doom, gloom or fear. If you dread the dentist and you are waiting at the front of a queue and you hear the words, 'Next please.' That pretty un-offensive verbal request may send you into a state of blind panic. It could also be true of waiting for your driving test, going for a parachute jump or diving in at the deep end of a swimming pool. But if you were waiting in line for a £100.00 pay out, 'Next please', would be the words you longed to hear!

It's the same thing when people say, 'I hate flying'. Believe me you don't hate flying. What you have a fear of is being 20,000 ft up in the air and 'not flying'? If the-captain announced, 'I'm sorry we are about to crash land.' You would shout 'I love flying, please let me fly!' Once again it's the context the words are used in that makes the difference.

If you were walking around a zoo with a friend and they said 'look over there, there's a lion!' you wouldn't be unduly worried. The same phrase used if you were both walking in a jungle would certainly have a different reaction.

So where is this all leading to in relation to aggression or violence? Well no greater or more powerful words are the 'speak' of intimidation or threats. From children to adults we all live at one time or another with a threat or an intimidating word. The problem is we really don't understand the difference between the two or understand why we feel fearful of these things.

In this chapter we will try to examine the 'speak' of the street in relation to violence.

So what is 'lntimidation'? Intimidation will always provide you with an option. For example, 'If you don't move, I'll punch your face in,' 'Give me £I,000 and I won't tell your wife you are having an affair.' The words will contain if, or else, unless or until. A mum will say to a child. 'You touch that again and I will punish you!' To intimidate is to issue some sort of warning to achieve a particular response. Nine times out of ten the person will not act on their words. People regularly throw intimidating remarks around all the time. The words become cheap. 'Don't touch my car or I'll kill you,' is a pretty profound statement but very few thank God actually mean those words!

We must realise intimidating people is just another form of bullying and we must not lose sight of this. Most intimidators wont follow up the threats unless it's some sort of legal matter, unpaid bills, council tax etc. Some people live their whole life under the threats of intimidation. Women in violent marriages, children who are abused, employees working for a bullying boss and so on.

A lot of people can intimidate to give them a protective fence around themselves. Some as discussed elsewhere can back up their threats, others can't. Those that can't rely on their intimidating tactics to protect them. Using these tactics can also get you what you want or control another person.

In sport these scare tactics can give an individual or team an edge to win. I remember reading about Liverpool football legend Tommy Smith. He had a reputation on the field for being a 'hard man' and it was no false label in his case. He intimidated many a player and put them totally out of their stride. Once ex-Leicester player Frank Worthington recalled how he had gone past Smith on two occasions earlier on in a game. Worthington was a great ball player and dribbler. After the second time Smith came up behind him and snarled in his ear, 'Do that again son and I'll break your f ----- g back!' Needless to say Worthington drifted out of the game. Smith's tactic worked.

I could recount many examples but I'm sure you get the picture. The rule is don't allow yourself to be intimidated. If you don't the person threatening will have no hold on you. This is true in the case of a blackmailer. Don't give them an edge so they have nothing to control you with. If you are in the position of being blackmailed, come clean and the blackmailer's hold is broken and they will go away. Be warned pay money once, you will pay it again and again. Don't do it.

If people shout an intimidating remark at us, our bodies immediately go into survival mode. Adrenalin courses through our veins, heart rate goes up, we break into a sweat, our breathing quickens. All these and more we mistake for fear. When this happens, check yourself and the situation. Are you in immediate danger, are there words going to hurt you, will you have to physically defend yourself? Evaluate the moment and react accordingly. Don't let fear or blind panic grip you. Think rationally and you will be able to deal with the situation.

The major problem is our minds are masters of conjuring up the worst case scenarios. If the person using intimidatory tactics has a reputation for Violence then we tend to believe they mean it when they say *'I'm going to tear your head off if you don't move out of the way!'* It can be a frightening occurance and when the fear factor is introduced we do-not think logically. Please remember words are only words and they cannot physically harm you, they will only do so if you allow them to get a grip on you and run wild through the corridors in your mind.

What about a threat? How is it different to intimidation? A threat gives no option. 'I'm going to kill you!' 'You're about to die!' When I next see you I'm going to shoot you! A threat gives you it straight but again most threats don't come to anything. Celebrities, politicians and people in promanent positions suffer threats all the time. Sure they have to be reported and taken seriously but as I mentioned most come to nothing. For the average person though being threatened can be an extremely scary and traumatic experience.

Anonymous threats can be a truly unpleasant experience. Whether received in a letter form or phone call, they can be very upsetting. Try to remember though a long distance threat is again very rarely followed up. It is a scare tactic, that gives the 'threatener' a sick rush of pleasure and satisfaction. Never forget they have chosen to be anonymous because they are cowardly and would never say the things they have mentioned to you face to face.

The 'In your face' threat should be taken more seriously. Why? Because this person has hid nothing from you. They are facing you down, maybe in the presence of witnesses and this doesn't faze them whatsoever. They have still openly made their threat.

If this threat has come after a long spell of previous intimidation, then take it serious, it means this person is running out of options and getting desperate. Desperate people take desperate measures, violent measures if need be.

The best way to deal with this is to deal with it there and then, don't allow the threat to hang in the air. Facing up to a threat demands a lot of courage but it is better to get the outcome over with now than have days or weeks of uncertainty waiting for a 'visit' or looking over your shoulder every minute.

If you feel the threat is serious, go to the police and voice your concern and get help. If you can't get any joy, my suggestion is to confront this person and 'settle the matter', how you do it I am not at liberty to suggest, but I guarantee this option is better than living in fear for weeks or months on end.

Remember the intimidator, blackmailer, etc only has power or a hold on you if you allow them. Do not give them a mental ledge to perch on, knock them off straight away and defeat their plan. Yes it takes courage but it is the quickest method of claiming back your normal life again.

Something else we must also consider is why we received the threat. Have we done this person wrong in some way? Do you know the person? Is it a friend, a family member, work colleague or neighbour? it could be a total stranger that you may have inadvertently upset. (e.g. cut up in your car, we jumped in front of in a queue etc) If you realise it's your fault, try and rectify the situation. Let's give you an example. You are in a crowded pub and you accidently knock the arm of a guy next to you, spilling his beer over his shirt. He whirls around and confronts you spewing out threats and obscenities. Try to calm the situation, apoligize, offer to buy him another drink. Ignore the initial burst of outrage, as discussed earlier some people just live on a knife edge. If this individual keeps ranting on and cursing you, say in a firm and calm manner, *'Look I've offered a drink, I can't be fairer than that'*, and walk away. It's best to leave the explosive area, because this situation is now deteriorating down the old familar path to violence. If you are perceptive of the signs, as I hope you are by now, we are heading for a pointless and stupid physical encounter. Leaving the scene may diffuse the situation. If your ego is so fragile that you can't but push the matter, then this book hasn't been of any help to you! Even if you know you could punch this guy's lights out, what is the point bringing a shed load of grief on yourself?

If when you have walked, the guy pursues you, then prepare to keep your distance and be prepared for the physical if you can't get away. Remember now in this instance you have no choice and if you have to defend yourself, be first, hit hard and fast with a pre-emptive strike and get away. Realise this last part of the scenario you couldn't avoid but before hand you had ample opportunity to make an escape route.

People in this day and age randomly spew out all sorts of intimidation and, threats without even thinking about what they're saying. You have to learn to let these remarks dissolve past you like water off a duck's back.

If somebody shouts out 'W--k-r' at you, don't let it faze you unless of course you are one! Talk is cheap, it's only hurtful if you allow it to be. If you work in the door supervisors world, in pubs and clubs, being called all sorts of names, being threatened etc is par for the course. These people just let it go over their head. They will not react unless they feel they are in physical danger. Some 'brainless individuals' think fronting out a doorman or 'throwing insults' at them make them some sort of hardcase. Most door personel are trained to only react when a person makes a physical move. The majority of these 'hardcases' won't make the move or over step the mark. For the average person being verbally abused and threatened is not on the daily agenda, that's why it can be so disturbing.

In my Martial Arts classes we practise verbal aggression de-escalation techniques. Where you re-create scenarios where one person will shout and snarl abuse at another, being as crude or insulting as they wish. This helps the other individual learn to let this abuse go over their head and not be fearful of it, but just accept it as part and parcel of the modern street thug. It is a powerful exercise, that is highly recommended for anybody that has trouble with verbal confrontation. Never forget the old saying 'stick and stones may break my bones, but names will never hurt me'.

Examples of street speak

a) 'What are you f ----- g looking at?

b) 'Are you f ----- g looking at me?'

c) 'What's your problem, pal?'

d) 'You looking for trouble?'

e) 'What you say, well, l'm f ----- g talking to you?'

f) 'You got a f ----- g problem with me?'

g) 'You do that again and you'll get a f ----- g slap'

h) 'Ow, w ---- r get out of the way'

i) 'You know me? Well? Do you want a go then do you?

j) 'You're looking at my Mrs. Well I asked you a question?'

k) 'Do I know you pal? Have you got a problem with me?'

The above examples are all entry techniques used by the aggressive street thug. They are used to see your reaction and close the distance on you. Beware of this. Do not get fixated by their dialogue otherwise you will not see them line you up for a strike. Remember the dialogue is meaningless, it is just a pre-cussor for violence. To learn more about this read Geoff Thompson's *'3 second Fighter'* or Jamie O'Keefe's *'Pre-emptive strikes for winning fights'*.

I have found most people even many Martial Artists will not have a clue how a street predator will use dialogue to set you up for an attack. If you don't read body language, understand street speak or attack ritual all the fighting skills in the world will stand for nothing, you will not get a chance to use them. So start learning about 'verbal aggression' and tame it, so again it becomes an impotent weapon that your aggressor cannot use against you.

Chapter 22
'The evil that men (and women) do'

This chapter was really an after thought when I had finished this book. In an ideal world I wouldn't have had to write it. But then in an ideal world there wouldn't be a need for this book at all! Unfortunately this is not the case, which this chapter will illustrate.

Whilst closing this book I noticed numerous 'pieces' in local and national newspapers within the space of a month that graphically summed up the type of people and violence which we have examined throughout the text.

It's easy sometimes if you read this type of book in the comfort of your house, with the curtains pulled, light on and a steaming cup of tea by your side to forget we are talking about 'real people' and 'real violence'. The following random news items will give us a reality check and let us know that violence is around us on a regular and occuring basis. You can bet that everyone of the victims in these news clippings didn't expect to become a casualty of violence, aggression and even death!

'-Rape at the seaside' *A teenager was subjected to a terrifying rape ordeal in a children's playground. The rapist pounced from behind, forced the victim to the floor and raped her before running off.*

'Murder quiz' *A teenage boy is being questioned over the murder of a 30 year old woman who was found stabbed to death outside a local pub.*

Horror remand' *A teenager is accused of killing and burying a vicar. The vicar's severed limbs were discovered in a sports bag in a shallow grave.*

Mum's been killed' *Horror as a five year old boy saw his mother killed in a savage knife attack by her jealous farmer lover, who then committed suicide by stabbing himself in the heart.*

'Royal aid murders lover' *Jan Andrews was found guilty today of blugeoning her boyfriend with a cricket bat and then stabbing him repeatively with a carving knife.*

'Police rapist' *A police inspector was found guilty of raping two women whilst being let into their homes to investigate other incidents.*

'War hero hanged' *War hero Bill Clifford hanged himself after six months of torment and abuse by a gang of young thugs who terrorized him at his home.*

'Youth stabbed racist street attack' *A teenager needed emergency surgery for stab wounds inflicted by a mob who shouted racist abuse at him. He suffered horrific chest and stomach wounds.*

'Cop couple beat up girl' *A married police couple were convicted yesterday of attacking a woman neighbour who complained about loud music from their barbecue.*

'Appeal over knife point robbery' *A 10 year old child was approached by a man wielding a knife. He was pushed against a wall and punched and kicked before the assailent ran off.*

'Rape beast's victim number six' *A rape monster was being hunted after striking for the 6th time. The knife wielding brute gets close to his victims by chatting them up in bars and then pounces when the women leave the premises.*

'Teenager shot' *A teenager was shot six times with an air rifle at a school leaving party. The 15 year old boy was shot repeatedly in the back.*

'Yobs attack' *Police are hunting a gang of youths after a women was sexually assaulted. The yobs ages ranged from 11 to 15 years of age.*

'Snooker hall killer batters 2' *A savage killer was being hunted last night after a woman was murdered and another badly hurt in a shocking attack at a snooker hall.*

'Pshycho sir' *Obsessed Brit teacher guns down girl pupil, 19, then kills himself.*
'Monster step dad' *He killed wife and four kids and had sex with the eldest*
'Axe fiend butchers boss ban' *A murder hunt was launched yesterday after a wealthy businessman was found with an axe buried in his head.*

'Man's inhumanity to man, makes countless thousands mourn'
Robert Burnes.

Chapter 23
How safe are you?

So how safe are you from the likelyhood of facing violence in your everyday life? Well obviously this will depend on a number of factors.

One could be your job. If you work as a policeman or in the security business then the likelyhood could be reasonably high. If you are a business person that has to travel to foreign countries then you could be high risk. Some jobs that don't seem dangerous by nature can have it's share of violent or aggressive moments, i.e. A&E worker, paramedic, traffic warden, DSS employee, tax office worker, job centre employee. In the line of work these people can certainly find themselves facing danger through aggressive, unhappy and disgruntled individuals. How does your job stand up to a safety check? What risks do you take in a day? When do you feel vulnerable or uneasy? I'm sure every job carries some element of risk and it may be judged on a scale of I to I0. If you are unhappy with a situation at work where you feel at risk, then don't hesitate to bring it to the managements attention. Don't just let it carry on or accept it. Employer and employee both have a responsibility for safety in the workplace. If your job is high risk then try to do everything possible to be well prepared using good pro-active tactics.

If you live in a high crime inner city area, the chances of being a victim of a robbery, mugging or assault may be considerably higher than if you live in the leafy suburbs. Living in bedsit land, hostels or rented accomodation can bring problems of burglary, strangers wondering around, poor security etc, and so it goes on.

Lifestyle has a lot to do with the likelyhood of running into violence or not. Of course as mentioned elsewhere in this book anybody, anywhere anytime can be a victim, but the key is to try and cut down the risks and make yourself a hard target..

Obviously life consists of risks in one form or another everyday and we cant wrap everybody up in cotton wool. Also wouldn't life be boring without risk? The key though is to be well prepared and adequately trained to minimise and cope with hazard.

A parachute jump is a big risk but when you are taught to do this you are trained fully in safety procedures before you attempt it, you minimise the dangers.

Throughout this book along with exploring man's violent nature, we have looked at how to minimise dangers. To 'nip it in the bud' and prevent escalation of a situation.

You must examine yourself and see if you are a high risk target or a walking victim.

How you carry yourself, speak, conduct yourself speaks volumes about you and can go a long way to determining whether you will be a victim. If you are the sort of person that sees no danger anywhere, or ignores warning signals, you are going to have a problem. If you can see no wrong in anybody or are over-trusting you will fall foul to the street predator. They will sniff you out from a distance and close in for 'the kill'.

Being aware of the dangers out there, being alert and perceptive of changing circumstances and having acceptance of violent crime happening to anybody, anytime, anywhere can go a long way to reducing the chances of your being a victim.

Yes you may want to take up a martial art or self protection system to give you confidence and physical skills but I would rather tell you how to avoid potentially dangerous situations as your first tactic rather than show you the mechanics of a good punch.

Real fighting as explained in my previous books, is not like TV or cinema fights, it's not like our school play ground scraps, or like a rehearsed and choreographed martial arts demonstration. It's not even like the mixed martial arts and limited rules fights that are so popular at present.

If you wish to learn to defend yourself in reality for street protection then contact either. The British Combat Association 0532 429 686 or The Self Defence Association 01709 710 489. These two associations will give you names and details of genuine registered self protection Instructors in your area that teach the whole gamut of a good and realistic self protection programme. They will not confuse martial arts, martial sports or anything else with street defence. You will get the 'real deal'.

Remember fighting skills are no different to any other skills, you will have to invest time in getting them right so they are instinctive and reactive. There are no quick-fix systems, no killer arts, or 5 easy lesson methods. But a little time spent in a good system can give you a lot of benefits and confidence.

But lets not forget the theme of this chapter, how hard a target are you to prevent a violent crime being perpetrated on your being.

Let's take a small test and be honest with your answers to this safety questionnaire. Answer yes, no or sometimes.

Risk assessment questionnaire
1.   Do you regularly visit night clubs and bars?
2.   Do you walk home on your own after a night out?
3.   Do you get heavily intoxicated each time you go out?
4.   Do you daydream in public?
5.   Do you always keep a check on your wallet/handbag?
6.   Do you park your vehicle in a well lit area?
7.   Do you wear expensive jewellery?
8.   Do you wear offensive or provocative clothing?
9.   Are you racist?
10. How often do you use ATM machines?
11. Do you hitch hike?
12. Do you wear a walkman whilst jogging in the park?
13. How often do you permit strangers into your house?
14. Do you provide personal information over the phone to a stranger?
15. Do you fall asleep on public transport?
16. Do you get into verbal disputes with strangers?
17. Do you suffer from road rage?
18. Have you got a short fuse?
19. Do you fly off the deep end at an insult or put down?
20. Have you got a problem with Authoritive figures?
21. Do you voice your opinions in a loud and tactless manner?

22.   Do you walk along with your hands in your pockets and head down?

23.   Does your job entail handling large amounts money?

24.   Does your job entail you travelling to foreign countries?

25.   Does your job entail you visiting potentially unsavoury areas or entering homes of strangers?

This is by no means an exhaustive list, it is a general overview. How did you do? If you answered yes to the majority of questions, you may want to review your life style and if you can't or won't chance it beware you are in a high risk bracket. If you were being insured against a 'violent attack' on the above questionnaire you would be paying a large premium. I know you cant go living behind closed doors all our lives or cowering at our shadows but we must work to have a sub conscious awareness of things around us, so that we can certainly enjoy life to the full but cut down the chances of running into violence. 'We all have a habit of looking back in hindsight let's make a habit out of looking in foresight for this is the smarter option'

Epilogue

Man has achieved much in his time on this planet. He has accomplished so many great feats. Look at the history books to see the many truly brilliant things that has changed the course of time. Space travel, telecommunication, Internet the motor car. Fantastic architecture, art, feats of incredible fitness and endurance, scientific discovery and much, much more. Man is truly a creative creature but on the flip side of the coin he is also a destructive one. As mentioned through history is search of power and glory he has caused mass destruction and bloodshed. Not only has he destroyed fellow man, he is slowly but surely savaging the planet he lives on. Global warming, atomic waste, ozone deteriation, rain forest rape and the hunting and extinction of entire species of wildlife, plant life and nature.

As brilliant as man is, he is also a flawed creature. He has killed more people in the name of religion and peace. Hitler nearly annihilated the Jewish population for his own selfish and misguided ways and beliefs.

Countries have warred continually spilling blood on their lands, leaving starving, homeless and totally ruined people, homesteads and cities.

Man is a serial killer, a pshyopath, a random mass murderer, a stalker, a wife beater, a child molester, a thug, a mutilator, a cannibal, a spontaneous and random perpetrator of violent attacks and aggression. This is a sad fact and I can only hope that somewhere along the way soon we realise that we only have one life and why should we spend our days hating, dispising and abusing our own kind. It is a complete waste of time and there are so many better things to be doing. The world has some wonderful places to be seen and fantastic people to be met. Don't dwell on the dark side otherwise when you do decide to seek the light you will not remember where it is.

This book has explored that dark side of the human being. We are all guilty of having visited that dark side at one or more times in our lives and no doubt no matter how hard you try somewhere along the line you will encounter one of lifes dark individuals, hopefully this text has given you a better understanding of their nature and prepare you for this encounter. These lessons take time to learn, it has taken me the best part of 30 years to understand and absorb what I have written about here. Hopefully it won't take you that amount of time but there are no real short cuts to properly achieving anything.

Zig Ziglar a famous American inspirational speaker once visited the Washington Monument with some friends, when a tour guide announced, 'Ladies and gentlemen, there is currently a 2 hour wait to take the life to the top'. Then he paused, smiled and added, 'However, there is no wait should you desire to take the stairs!' There are no lifts to the top, if you want to get there you've got to take the stairs. How many you're willing to climb, determines how high you'll go!

Remember also the motto used earlier on 'walk softly and carry a big stick', well if all else fails and you can't avoid trouble make sure the stick is a f ----- g big one! Finally as we have trawled through man's bad side, he still thankfully also has as much good to offer. Be safe and sound.

Kevin O'Hagan Aug 2001

Footnote:

During the completion of this book, the terrible and tragic events of the terrorist attacks on the U.S.A. happened. This brought home the hardhitting fact of the scale of violence and destruction man is still capable of and willing to inflict on fellow human beings with some crazy and misguided cause. Terrorism is another face of violence that must also be addressed. I hope no-one will ever have to face the scale of disaster that the United States did. I have visited the states on many occasions ans know many people there. My thoughts and prarers are with them all.

Sept 2001

BRISTOL KEMPO GOSHIN JUTSU COMBAT ACADEMY
SENSEI KEVIN O'HAGAN'S TRAINING VIDEOS AND BOOKS

BOOKS
I Thought You'd Be Bigger £I4 (inc. P&P)
 The small person's guide to fighting back
2. In Your Face - Close Quarter Fighting £I4 (inc. P&P)
3. Grappling with Reality £I4 (inc. P&P)

VIDEOS
1. OFFICAL GRADING SYLLABUS
2. IMPACT JU JUTSU VOL. I
'Training and Conditioning for Combat'
3. IMPACT JU JUTSU VOL II
'A full array of advanced exercises for combat conditioning'
4. IMPACT JU JUTSU VOL Ill
'Innovative and Functional Training and Conditioning Methods'
5. DOWN AND OUT VOL. I
'Standing to Floor Ju Jutsu Techniques'
6. DOWN AND OUT VOL. II
'Advanced Standing to Floor Techniques'
7. FISTFUL OF DYNAMITE (YAWARA BO)
'Dynamic techniques using this small but highly effective weapon'
8. WEAPON DISARMING
'Brutal and effective techniques for disarming an array of modern and makeshift weaponry'
ALL VIDEOS ARE INSTRUCTED BY SENSEI KEVIN O'HAGAN AND ARE AVAILABLE AT £I5 (INC. P&P)
PLEASE PHONE 0117 952 5711 FOR DETAILS

visit Web -Site on www.bristolgoshinjutsu.com
Or E-Mail Cannon@BristolCity24.freeserve.co.uk
Kevin O'Hagan also appears as a guest writer on GEOFF THOMPSON'S website www.geoffthompson.com

KEMPO GOSHIN JUTSU

Kempo Goshen Jutsu is a modem art in its outlook and practice. Its roots are in the ancient Japanese Ju Jutsu system, art of the Samurai Warrior. Ju Jutsu can be termed the "Grandfather" art for modem systems like Karate, Judo and Aikido. These arts are modem (developed 1930's). Ju Jutsu is centuries old. It is a battlefield art solely for self protection, there are no sporting elements.

Kempo Goshin Jutsu keeps the traditional roots and discipline of Ju Jutsu, but recognises time change and so does the threat of violence. We take a modem view to deal with the types of dangers we face today. Kempo Goshin Ju Jutsu is down to earth in its approach, no mystical mumbo-jumbo or outdated impractical techniques.

It has vast syllabus of techniques - punches, kicks, strikes, throws, locks, pressure points, chokes, strangles, groundwork, weapon defences, use of traditional and modem weaponry and makeshift weaponry from everyday articles. It deals with the mental conditioning and physiology of facing violence.

Kempo Goshin Jutsu is flexible enough for anyone to practice - young, old, men, women, fit, unfit, disabled, whoever. We can teach everybody something useful and maybe life saving.

We also train in Competitive Submission Wrestling, Brazilian Jujutsu and "No Holds Barred" Vale Tudo for Mixed Martial Arts Tournaments. Full contact use of the focus pads, Thai pads and shields along, with hard conditioning exercises and grappling drills prepare you for the ultimate test.

ACADEMY INSTRUCTORS - Combat Ju jutsu/Self Protection
Kevin O'Hagan 6 th Dan -
Mike Griffin   2 nd Dan -
Paul Flett 1st Dan
Matt Sperring 1st Dan
Rob Cannon 1st Dan (Club Secretary)
Phil Davis 1st Dan
Andrew Wintle 1st Dan
PRESENT COMPETING TEAM
Kevin O'Hagan, Paul Flett, Rob Cannon, Matt Sperring, Ross Mackenzie, Steve Thomas, Mark Clemmings, Phil Davis

BRISTOL GOSHIN JUTSU COMBAT ACADEMY TRAINS AND TEACHES

STREET SELF DEFENCE

COMBAT JUJUTSU

SUBMISSION GRAPPLING

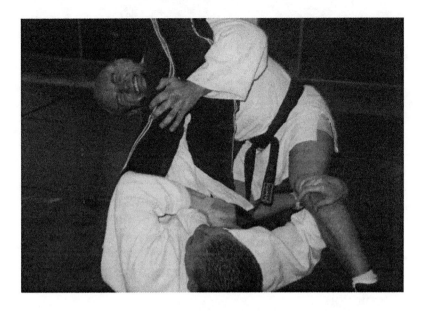

VALE TUDO

Adverts

Will the reader please note that the following advertising section of the book is included to let you know of other Self Protection related merchandise.

You the reader, have not been charged for the printing or paper used in this section. The cost for this has been absorbed by New Breed Publishing.

The price that you have paid for this publication is for the knowledge, information and advice given by Kevin O'Hagan throughout the rest of this book.

Thank you

VIDEOS
TO
BUY

By

KEVIN O'HAGAN

'FISTFUL OF DYNAMITE'

**Yawara-Bo is an excellent and compact little weapon
That can be an instant source of painful control.**

**Anybody of any age can learn how to use this
Lethal little stick, quickly with good effect!**

BRISTOL GOSHIN JUTSU
COMBAT ACADEMY
PRESENTS

NEW VIDEO RELEASES
Featuring Kevin O'Hagan 6th Dan

"FISTFUL OF DYNAMITE"
YAWARA-BO TECHNIQUES

60 mins of dynamic techniques using this small but
highly effective weapon...plus substitute makeshift
Yawara-bo's from everyday articles...!

Excellent value at **£14.00**

(*Please add £1.00 for postage and packing*)

Please make cheques payable to "**Kevin O'Hagan**"
and post to

23 Chester Road, St.George, Bristol BS5 7AX
Telephone: 0117-952 5711

Genuine 60 minutes of action guaranteed

'Down & out'

Grappling and groundwork is the 'in thing'
Within Martial arts at present.

**If you want to expand your knowledge within this area,
this video is for you.**

**It's loaded with basic and advanced
throws and takedowns, with a
Multitude of ground submissions and finishes.**

"DOWN AND OUT"
STANDING TO FLOOR JU-JUTSU
TECHNIQUES

Featuring Kevin O'Hagan 6th Dan

"50" Throws and takedowns with a multitude of finishing holds and submissions!! Hard to find information and techniques on just one tape (60 mins)

Excellent value at **£14.00**

(*Please add £1.00 for postage and packing*)

Please make cheques payable to "**Kevin O'Hagan**"
and post to

23 Chester Road, St.George, Bristol BS5 7AX
Telephone: 0117 952 5711

Genuine 60 minutes of action guaranteed

A new video from Kevin O'Hagan
"DOWN AND OUT" Vol 2

More dynamic Strikes, throws and submission techniques.

Learn advanced combinations, joint locks, leg locks, chokes, strangles, and much more. This tape is loaded with first class technique.

Modern Combat Jujitsu at it's best

Price £15 inclusive of Post and Packing
Contact Kevin O'Hagan for more details.

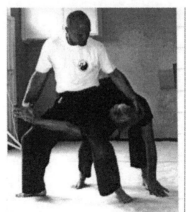

"If I wanted to learn something new – this is the video that I would choose. In fact, Kevin O'Hagans videos are the most used tapes in my own personal collection. I have not released any videos of my own because I do not feel I could improve on Kevins instructional tapes!"

Jamie O'Keefe 6th Dan
'Hall of Fame Awardee 1999' & 2001
'Founder Fellow of the Society of Martial Arts'.
'Self Protection instructor for Seni 2000, 2001
Birmingham Expo'

IMPACT JUJUTSU Vol II

The follow on to 'Impact Jujutsu'

This time learn advanced drills, exercises and Conditioning routines. Some unique to Kevin O'Hagan And his Ju Jutsu system.

See it all put together in Freestyle all out sparring too!

IMPACT JUJUTSU Vol II
Out now!
The new follow up video to the successful
IMPACT JUJUTSU Vol 1

This time **Kevin O'Hagan, 6th Dan Jujutsu,** and his senior instructor Paul Flett, take you through a full array of advanced exercises including:
Conditioning, Speed drills, Throws, Padwork, Groundwork drills, Boxing, Vale Tudo (Sparring) and much more...

This tape is a must for anybody serious about training for peak fitness and all round Cross training skills.

Enjoy and learn from this informative and exciting new video available **only** from Kevin O'Hagan.

Excellent value at **£14.00**
(Please add £1.00 for postage and packing)

Please make cheques payable to "**Kevin O'Hagan**" and post to
23 Chester Road, St.George, Bristol BS5 7AX

Telephone: 0117-952 5711

IMPACT JUJUTSU Vol III

Book review by Geoff Thompson.
Grad. SMA. FSMA

I Thought You'd Be Bigger
A Small person's guide to Fighting back.

Kevin O'Hagan is one of the up-and-coming stars of the martial arts in the Nineties. Author of many thought-provoking articles and now his first martial arts book, 'I thought You'd Be Bigger – A Small Person's Guide to Fighting Back' he is one of the highest ranked Ju-Jitsu players in the country today having recently acquired his 5th Dan. This book is a result of his life work in Ju-Jitsu and is a very worthy read for anyone, large or small, that is interested in bettering their chances of survival on the pavement arena.

You know, I've worked with violence and violent people all of my adult life and I've learned an awful lot about the human experience and the capacity that our species has to destroy its self over as little as a spilled drink in a bar or eye contact across a busy street: even minor traffic incidents these days seem to be justification enough, to some, to take the life of another human being-it is a hugely violent age that we find seem to find our selves in.

Because our problem on this spinning planet is large, one would automatically presume that it would take a person of equal proportion-i.e. very big- in the physical sense, to deal with or neutralise the problem.
Not so!

At least not from my experience. I have dealt with thousands of violent altercations, I have also had to deal with big men (the odd big woman too!) and faced many life threatening situations, because of this people, when they meet me for the first time, will invariably say in an almost disappointed tone **'Oh! I thought you'd be bigger**.

What a great title for a book on self defence, if only Kevin O'Hagan hadn't thought of it first and beaten me to the post (Damn!)

Joking aside, it is a brilliant title for a book on self-defence and I can think of no man better qualified to write such a text as my good friend and colleague Kevin O'Hagan.
Not only is it a great title it is also a great book for anyone that thinks size, or lack there off, has any debilitating qualities when it comes to protecting your self and those that you love.

I can tell you categorically that the most ferocious fighters that I have ever worked with have been physically small, like Kevin, but absolute dynamite when the fuse was lit.

I have known Kevin for quite a few years now, not only is he a very personable man he is also a first rate martial artist, one of the few that I really admire and one of even fewer high graded martial artists in Britain that is not afraid to don the white belt and learn off just about anyone that has something of worth to teach.

He is a realist, one of the leaders in the new age of realism, he talks the talk and he walks the walk so I heartily recommend and endorse this text to anyone, of any size or stature, that wants to be better prepared when the metaphoric 'big bad wolf tries to blow your house down.

This is a great book, buy, read it and be bigger for the experience.

Geoff Thompson, Coventry 1998.

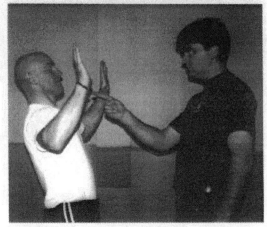

I THOUGHT
You'd be
BIGGER !

A SMALL PERSONS
guide to
FIGHTING BACK
by Kevin O'Hagan

Ever feel inferior or intimidated by a large person?
Maybe you have been bullied by such a person?
Maybe you have been the victim of violence 'offered' by a big aggressive assailant?
Or maybe you just live in fear of being attacked by someone bigger than yourself?
Our society has conditioned us to think BIG is strong and dangerous and small is weak, defenceless...
Time to re-think, the small person can fight back and win!
In "I thought you'd be bigger", find out the crucial mental and physical elements needed to survive a violent encounter with the 'big guy.'
Kevin O'Hagan a 5th Dan black belt in Ju Jutsu, gives you his valuable insights from *22 years experience of the Combat Arts* on this essential but over-looked topic in the world of the fighting Arts.
This book contains much sought after and hard to find information on personal self-protection for the **'little people.'**

A real lifesaver!

ISBN 0 9517567 7 X

£12.99

New Breed Publishing
P.O.Box 511
Dagenham
Essex RM8 3NF
England

ISBN 0-9517567-7-X

9 780951 756775

In Your Face
'CLOSE QUARTER FIGHTING'
by
Kevin O'Hagan

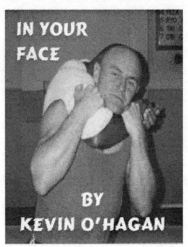

£ 14

from
NEW BREED
Or even better
Buy it direct from Kevin O'Hagan
And ask him to autograph it!

Your Advert, Book, Video or Company could be featured here plus in our other books

----

Foreword by Jamie O'Keefe
'In your face'
'Close Quarter fighting'

When I was approached by Kevin O'Hagan to do a foreword for this book I had to think long and hard about it for a tenth of a second. That's the time it took me to give him my reply, which was yes! And honoured I am that he asked me to.

It shows me that my opinion is regarded as of importance, which gives a special kind of feeling. Although I have written five self protection related books myself; that's an area where I write what I like with complete control over the content matter and the worst thing that could happen is that if people don't like what I have to say, they don't buy my books. Fortunately that's not the case.

Writing this foreword presents a complete different scenario and responsibility. I am not putting the world to rights, giving my opinions and philosophies for the reader to agree or disagree with. My task here is to validate the accuracy of the facts, advice and information given within this publication combined with my own personal testimonial of its author Kevin O'Hagan. With this in mind I now put my finger to the keyboard and hope that I can do justice to such a worthwhile publication.

I think that it can be fair to say that I know Kevin well. In fact I have personally known Kevin for around 20 years since we were both training in traditional martial arts; both searching for that something that seemed to be missing from our respective arts. That something was and is, called 'Self Protection.'

We each followed different paths in our journey; testing, trying, analysing, every aspect of the martial and related fighting systems until we each individually found what we were looking for.

We both ended up at the rank of 6th dan Black belt and are now regarded as premier league players in the world of self protection. At this level you instinctively know what's 'real' and what's bull!

Kevin is as real as 'real' comes. He knows his stuff. He lives, breathes and eats self protection and is one of the most dedicated self protection participants and instructors that I know of.

Kevin is a serious player who I would certainly like to have by my side if faced with an ugly encounter that I felt uncomfortable dealing with alone. Beside him being a superb martial artist and excellent self protection instructor, he is a really respectful nice guy.

What more can I really say other than that this is the second book that he has written and I would have been proud to have released either of these titles myself. 'In your face' is a superb book which I advise you to read and digest. I am not going to spoil the plot by giving you a breakdown of the books contents because you really do need to read it for yourself. What I will say though is that if you do read it thoroughly. You will find something that might just possibly tip the scales in your favour if you are ever faced with a serious threatening encounter. Just ask yourself now, do you feel 100% comfortable that you can deal with the 'worst of the worst' of situations staring you in the face?

If you rate yourself at 99% capable or below, read this book to gain the other missing percent. Your life and that of your loved ones deserve that extra bit of security.

This is another great book by Kevin and I am proud to associate my name with him.

Stay safe and train as you live.

Jamie O'Keefe 1998. F.S.M.A.
(Founder fellow of the Society of Martial Arts)

If you enjoyed this book why not order the other titles currently available from

**Jamie O'Keefe
Kevin O'Hagan
Alan Charlton
Steve Richards**

THEY ARE AN IDEAL PRESENT
IF YOU WANT TO
GIVE SOMETHING DIFFERENT AND SPECIAL

If you borrowed this book and would like your
own copy, give
Kevin O'Hagan a call on
0117 952 5711

(Get Kevin to sign and personalise your copy)

**Your Advert, Book, Video or Company
could be featured here
plus in our other books**

Would you like to write a book or become an author?

NEW BREED PUBLISHING
Turned this book idea into reality
For Kevin O'Hagan

If you have an idea for a book and would like
to see it in print

Give us a call for an initial discussion.

- Please do not send us any manuscripts or ideas without prior arrangement

Contact New Breed Publishing
www.newbreedbooks.co.uk

NEW BREED PUBLISHING

- Do you want to advertise in our books?
- Do you want to become an outlet for our books?
- Do you want to become an agent for us?
- Do you want to join our mailing list?
- Do you want to organise a course or Seminar with one of our Authors?
- Do you want to speak to or meet one of our Authors?

We can work together!

New Breed Publishing

Or via Email on **info@newbreed.worldonline.co.uk**

www.newbreedbooks.co.uk

Or in writing to

New Breed
Po box 511
Dagenham
Essex RM9 5DN
England

PREVENT YOURSELF FROM BECOMING A VICTIM
'Dogs don't know Kung Fu'
A guide to Female Self Protection
By Jamie O'Keefe £ 14 including post & packing
Never before has Female Self Protection used this innovative approach to pose questions like. Why do Rapist's Rape? Why are Women abused? Why do Stalkers Stalk? This book takes a look at all Simple, Serious, and Life threatening aspects of Self Protection that concern us daily, along with **PREVENTION** of Child abuse and Child Abduction, Emotional cruelty, Telephone abuse, Road rage, Muggers, Date rape, Weapon attacks, Female abduction, Sexual Assault & Rape, Self defence law, and what it will allow us to do to protect ourselves, plus much more. With over 46,500 words, 77 pictures and 200 printed pages 'Dog's Don't Know Kung fu' is a no nonsense approach to women's self defence. It covers many realistic scenarios involving Children's abduction as well as typical attacks on women. Besides quoting actual events, the book explains how to avoid trouble and how you should react if you get into a situation.
This book is a 'must read' for all women and parents.
It is also important for teenage women, but, due to some of its graphic depiction's of certain incidences, parents should read it first and decide if it's suitable for their child.

Foreword

Dogs don't know kung fu

I'm not usually known for writing forewords to books on self protection, and not because I'm afraid of competition, on the contrary, the more people offering good advice in the fight for better protection be better:- rather its because most of what I read on the subject is crap.

I would never be happy putting my name to something that does not represent my own views, and that's putting it mildly. Not only are the proffered 'self defence' techniques in these manuals unlikely, they are also, very often, dangerous and opinionated.

I have written some 20 books to date on self protection and related subjects so you'd think that there would be very little left for me to learn. I rarely if ever find a manuscript that inspires me or even one that offers something new, a fresh perspective, an innovative approach.

Jamie's book did all the latter. He offered inspiration and sensible (and in retrospect, obvious) solutions to the many enigmatic 'grey areas' that had long perplexed me, a so called expert.

Questions that I have been pondering upon for years were answered at the first reading of this text. So I not only commend Mr O'Keefe on writing probably the best self protection book for women on the market but I also thank him for filling in the gaps in what is, at best, a very intangible subject.

What makes this book even more unique is that Jamie is a veteran instructor with thousands of hours of women's self protection under his belt, he is also an empiricist in that he has put his training to work in real life situations. Now while this may not say a lot to the lay man/woman, to those in the know, it speaks volumes.

Most of the instructors out there teaching self protection have never been in a real situation and so garnish unreal scenarios with un-workable, hypothetical technique.

You will get no such balderdash from this cutting edge instructor. What is offered on the menu in this text will prepare you, of that I have no doubt.

Self protection in the very violent 20th century must now, out of necessity be viewed as an environmental seat belt, it can no longer be down graded as a recreational pastime that comes third down the list of priorities after basket weaving, people are being attacked and killed, every day of the week, in un-provoked, un-solicited and bloody attacks.

My advice to you the reader is to take on board what Jamie has to offer as preventive measures and make them part of your life. Being aware will help you to avoid the majority of attack scenarios, for those that fall outside the periphery of avoidance, the simple, yet effective physical techniques on offer in this book will, if employed with conviction, help to neutralise even the most ardent of attackers.

This is a great book that makes great sense.

The best of its kind.

Geoff Thompson. Coventry 1996

BOUNCERS - SECURITY
DOOR SUPERVISORS
THIS IS THE BOOK THAT TELLS IT ALL

No matter what position you hold in your workplace.
The actions of **Security** will affect your safety and that of the general public.

Do you really know all you should about
Door Supervisors?

Find out how much
Door supervisors
should know - but don't
know!
If you want professionalism
from your Door Supervisors,
you must read this book

If you want to become a Door Supervisor
You should read this book!
If you are a Door Supervisor, Security, or Bouncer,
You must have this book!
No matter how long you have worked the doors –
you will learn something from this book

Peter Consterdine said
'This book is a blueprint for the future'

Foreword

Old School – New School

Whether you want to call them Bouncers, Doormen or Door Supervisors, they are still the people with the most thankless job I know.

Constantly under pressure from their own employers, local authorities, the police and especially the general public, it is no wonder that on occasions their self control is taxed to its ultimate. At times, even the best can lose that fine sense of perspective that allows them, night after night to take the constant barrage of banal and often alcohol influenced verbals whilst still keeping the smile in place.

I'd like to think that even going back some 23 years when I first started working on the doors that I subscribed to the "**new school**" approach so creativity described in Jamie's latest book. At that time I weighed eleven and a half stone at six foot one and despite having been on the Gt. Britain and England Karate Teams for some years I knew my traditional marital arts had limited value in the very particular conditions one finds in a night-club.

My weapons were politeness, humour, intellect and large doses of patience and, at times, even larger doses of pre-emptive strikes when occasion demanded. I'm the first to admit, however, that the conditions which applied in the seventies are different to today.

I saw the change begin in the eighties when, as a club owner, it was apparent that the nature of violence, the carrying of weapons, even handguns and the influence of drugs, was going to exact a heavy toll and so it has.

Twenty years ago when someone threatened to come back and shoot me, I slept easy knowing that the next day he wouldn't even remember where he had been the night before - now you'd be reaching for the ballistic vest.

Gang warfare, drugs, control of doors, protection rackets are all now part of the club scene and in the middle is today's doormen. Some are corrupt, some are vicious, some are plain thick, but the majority are honest, well intentioned and keen to do a good job in the face at mounting pressure from many quarters and increased violence and all this with "officialdom" now peering over their shoulder.

Often lied to by the police as to their correct rights of self defence under the law. This book should re-educate people about not only the law, but the many other complex issues.

Expected to be amateur psychologists and perfect man managers versed in a whole range of conflict resolution skills, doormen are still on the 'front line', both male and female.

Door licensing schemes are supposedly the answer to the problems inherent in the profession, but they only go part way to solving many of the issues which still give cause for concern.

Old School, New School clearly defines the gulf between the two approaches as to how the work should be carried out and it should be obligatory reading not only for all door people, but also the police and anyone who has an interest in the leisure industry. By doing so they will get a very clear and honest idea about the difficulties of this work.

Old School, New School isn't just a book about doorwork. It is an effective manual on modern methods of conflict resolution. Over the past few years there has been a substantial rise in the number of companies specialising in delivering courses on conflict resolution in the workplace.
If you read this book you will have all the answers to the management of conflict and aggression.
Doormen have been doing this for years, the only difference being the fact that they have developed their skills from intuition and experience of interpersonal skills in often very violent and

aggressive environments.

Now we know that this is a science just as any other form of social interaction and **'Old School, New School'** sets out to educate on the complexities of what is required.

The book recognises, however, that learning these very specialised skills will still not be any guarantee that you can create a person who can be capable of operating in this increasingly dangerous environment. The job is harder now than it ever was and don't let anyone tell you otherwise. Doing this job puts you under a microscope and an official one at that. `Big Brother' most certainly watches over your shoulder and, many would submit, quite rightly so.

I know many doormen who should have no part to play in the industry and many people to whom the recent changes will be hard to adjust to. What I know for a certainty is that the inherent dangers of the work increase every year.

For those doormen and the people who control them to resist the pressure from others to become another drugs distribution outlet takes courage and confidence from everyone in the organisation. Many crumble and give in to the pressure and violence, but equally many don't and I hope that **Old School, New School** will give people not involved in this work, a clear insight for once, the dangers and complexity of the work. For those people who are in the thick of it, I believe that this book is a "blueprint" for the future.

Peter Consterdine

7th Dan Chief Instructor – British Combat Association

Author of :
The Modern Bodyguard
Fit to Fight
Streetwise

What makes tough guys tough?
The Secret Domain

WHAT MAKES

TOUGH GUYS
TOUGH
The Secret Domain
by Jamie O'Keefe

Exclusive interview with Roy Shaw on What Makes Tough Guys Tough

Written by Jamie O'Keefe

Jamie O'Keefe has interviewed key figures from boxing, martial arts, self-protection, bodyguards, doorwork, military, streetfighting and so on. Asking questions that others were too polite to ask but secretly wanted to know the answers.

Interviews include prize-fighter **Roy Shaw**, also **Peter Consterdine, Geoff Thompson,** and **Dave Turton** from the countries leading self-protection organisations 'The British Combat Association' and the 'Self Defence Federation.' Along with Boxing heroes **Dave 'Boy' Green** and East London's former Commonwealth Champion **'Mo Hussein.'** **Plus unsung heroes from the world of Bouncers, Foreign Legion, Streetfighters, and more.**

This book also exposes the Secret Domain, which answers the question 'What makes tough guys tough.'

Find out what some of the toughest guys on the planet have to say about 'What makes tough guys tough' and how they would turn you into a tough guy.

Available from NEW BREED at £ 14 inc p&p

FOREWORD
DAVID TURTON 7th DAN GOSHINKWAI COMBAT
SENIOR INSTRUCTOR..
BRITISH COMBAT ASSOCIATION

When I was asked by Jamie to write a foreword to this, his latest book, I was both pleased & honoured, and a little intimidated by the prospect.

The first seemingly obvious thing I did, was to read it..

Sounds obvious, but I mean **REALLY** read. On doing so, I found myself being drawn quite deeply into Jamie's thoughts and ideals.

Jamie tends to venture into fields that few, if any, other authors have entered. In doing so, he lays open many often-unanswered questions. He makes those of you-who have asked themselves these soul searching questions, feel that they are not alone.

Having known Jamie for more years than both of us care to remember, I have the advantage of being able to 'hear' his voice, whilst reading his words. I can hear the inflections that show his passion in his beliefs, and the sheer sense of honesty of his words.

Read this book with no other distractions, and give it the respect of doing so with your full attention. Only then the effort will be rewarded with the insight you will get.

I first met Jamie 0'Keefe around twenty years ago. I was a Guest Instructor on an All-Styles self-defence course, and Jamie was a participant on the course, a very noticeable one at that.

I thought here was a talented Karate-Ka, a bit brash, but Oh, so very eager to learn. He was mainly into what we thought of as 'Free-style' Karate back then, but searching for something more. His thirst for learning was nearly insatiable. His Black Belt status was of no real consequence to him. He simply wanted to get stuck in and learn.

He's still doing just that. ... **THE SAME ENTHUSIASM IS PARAMOUNT IN HIS WRITINGS.**

I have looked for a way to go past the usual platitudes, and try to give; what I feel is an honest appraisal of what I feel Jamie is trying to give.... Then it registered ... That's the word ... **HONEST**.. That's the man and his writings.

Jamie always 'tells it like it is'. No holds barred, and no respecter of the many fragile Egos so prevalent in the Martial Arts these days. In this, he ranks along my two other favourite HONEST Combat Authors ... Geoff Thompson and Peter Consterdine.

Don't read this book for 'ways to do it', Don't read this book and be offended by his honesty. Read it, because NOT to read it, will leave a massive hole in your understandings of the World of Man & Violence.

Make it part of your collection, but keep going back to it to read it again and again.

I RECOMMEND THIS BOOK,
I DON'T RECOMMEND MANY... '**READ IT**'

DAVID TURTON 7th DAN GOSHINKWAI COMBAT.

How would you like to be able to
Stop an attack in its tracks?

How would you also like to be able to do it
within a second or two?

How would you like to do it without even
having to draw a breath?

Finally, would you like to know what the
alternative to grappling is?

Then get

'Pre-emptive strikes for winning fights'
'The alternative to grappling'

by
Jamie O'Keefe

Pre-emptive strikes
for winning fights
'The alternative to grappling'

by
Jamie O'Keefe
£ 14 inc P&P
from
New Breed
Po Box 511
Dagenham, Essex RM9 5DN

Foreword
Pre-Emptive Strikes

On first meeting Jamie O'Keefe, I was struck by his warmth and humour. I was then struck by his fists, head, & knees... Having been on the receiving end (though thankfully only in training) I can attest to the extreme effectiveness of the techniques he teaches. However, as I got to know him better, I was even more impressed by his integrity, honesty and commitment to teaching. Like many of the finest instructors and toughest fighters, Jamie is a gentleman.

These days I consider Jamie a good friend, but that's not why I agreed to write this forward. I believe he writes some of the best material available on modern self-protection, material, which can be, quite literally, life-saving.
I am proud to be able to associate my name with such valuable work
So what is the value in devoting a whole book to the pre-emptive strike?

Be in no doubt that this is one of the most important concepts for personal protection you will ever learn. Over the years I have read about, trained with and worked the door with many individuals who have vast experience of real violence. Every single one of them *without exception* recommends and uses the pre-emptive strike as the prime tactic for self-protection when a physical assault seems inevitable.

This book thoroughly dissects the theory, training and practical application of the pre-emptive strategy. From legal and moral ramifications to pre-attack indicators, from action triggers to Jamie's unique 'Strike Storage & Retrieval System', this book is the most exhaustive, insightful and thought-provoking treatise on the subject I have yet seen.

The lessons contained within these pages were learned the hard way, with spilt, blood & broken bones - this book was written so you don't have to take that route.

Read, absorb, and live by Jamie's advice. You'll be stronger and safer for it.

When talk fails and escape is impossible or impractical, the pre-emptive strike is your best option. I'll let Jamie tell you why.

Simon James
Instructor, Close Quarter Combat Systems

Want to know what its like
when it really kicks off?

Forget the movies - this is the REAL world.

Jamie O'Keefe

www.newbreedbooks.co.uk

Thugs, mugs and violence
The story so far

In this true account of his journey, Jamie O'Keefe unveils the reality of living in the East End of London. From childhood to adult this compelling, harrowing and often highly amusing story tells of his encounters with streetfighting, crime, drugs, violence and the martial arts. It goes through the trials and tribulations of boyhood right through to his days of working on the door in the heart of London's nightlife. Read how each of his confrontations and experiences have played a major part in making him the well respected authority in the fighting arts that he is today.

This book is sure to intrigue and fascinate you so much it will be hard to put it down..

The names and places have been changed in order to protect the guilty

The late Reg Kray telephoned me from prison, after having just undergone eye surgery to talk through the foreword for the re-print of this book.

Due to time restraints and the restrictions that he is bound by, I asked him if he could sum up his thoughts, on this book in a lone paragraph, rather than a lengthy foreword. Although Reg has given me his consent to quote him in length on all the good things that he has said about this book. I have decided to just go with the lone paragraph which was written by Reg himself. *'Thugs mugs and violence'* now has a permanent place within the cell of Reg Kray and is also read by the other inmates.

Thank you Reg for you phone-calls, sometimes three a day, to share your thoughts, ideas, opinions and philosophies with me.

Your friend
Jamie

"Jamie's book 'Thugs, Mugs and Violence' is an insight into the violent times of today and should be read" **Reg Kray – Kray Twins**

Photograph kindly supplied to me for inclusion by Reg Kray

REG KRAY – 32 YEARS SERVED
1968 – 2000 HM Prison.

Foreword

When I was asked by Kevin to write the foreword to this, Kevin's third book, I was both honoured and surprised. Honoured, because it is a great privilege to write for such an esteemed leader in the field of self-protection. Surprised because, although I have trained and practised various styles for many years, the last four with the Bristol Goshin Jutsu Combat Academy, I am, by no means, an authority on self-protection or the martial arts. I was simply a student of Kevin's who happened also to be criminal defence lawyer. What then could l, a humble lawyer, possibly have to contribute to a book on self-protection by this renowned exponent of the art?

A clue was found in the foreword to Kevin's first book, I Thought you'd be Bigger, which along with his second book, In Your Face, holds pride of place on my bookshelf. In that book, Geoff Thompson, describing Kevin as a 'first rate martial artist' stated that Kevin was one of the few highly graded martial artists who is not afraid to learn from just about anyone that has something of worth to share. This insight into Kevin's personality is precisely what makes him a truly inspirable instructor and self-protection expert. Unlike many mainstream styles whose techniques would be more at home in 17th century Japan, Kevin looks to the streets and people of today's inner cities for inspiration for his own unique and brutally effective style.
Samurai swords do not feature greatly on the streets - bottles, knives and heavy boots do - and Kevin knows it! And unlike many other styles, Kevin doesn't teach techniques as individual acts, but rather he advocates a manner of self-protection that is both fluid and responsive to the environment.
Kevin refers to the techniques of his style as parts of a jigsaw puzzle, each piece (technique) part of a larger whole. If the attacker doesn't respond to one technique, then you move into another.

In this way, each of us was taught to respond to what was physically happening, not to hope that the attacker did this or that and execute the technique regardless. Again, this is the real world - no formal rituals, no time to think. Every technique that Kevin teaches is designed to deal with a real life, in your face, situation.

And with each technique that I learnt and practised, I could see, in my opponent, the faces of the defendants that I saw in court each day (no offence to any of my opponents intended!). And that's how I came to be asked to write this foreword.

You see, as a criminal defence, lawyer, I spent years in police stations, prisons and courts representing the very kind of people that Kevin's style is designed to defend against - real-life murderers, muggers, rapists and robbers. In the evenings, I would attend Kevin's classes and I would delight in telling him, just after he had demonstrated an attack and how to deal with it, 'Yeah, that's the kind of attack that my client used the other night on some poor bastard in the city centre'. I would delight in it because I knew that it meant that what we were doing was real. This wasn't 17th century Japan stuff. This was real-world, real-time self-protection. I'd be thinking that this is what could have happened to me last night if I'd been in the same place, at the same time, as the particular victim that my client had chosen. Kevin was an enthusiastic listener and was always very interested to know the details. Each day that I sat in court, I would hear tales of violence and intimidation perpetrated by thugs and muggers and every time I would hear the details of what they did, I could see in my mind how Kevin's style and training, had it been known to the victim, would have enabled him or her to turn that threat around and put the attacker on the back foot, (or indeed, as with most of Kevin's techniques, on the ground in pain!).

As a lawyer, I had the unique opportunity, unavailable to most students of self-protection, of spending hours talking with my clients, probing them on what they did, and how they chose their victim. And what I learnt from these people is what I can contribute to this book.

I can tell you, without hesitation, that there is not one technique that Kevin teaches that is unrealistic nor one attack that he drills each student, or reader of this book, to protect him or herself against, that has not been used in real life somewhere on the streets of Britain last night or that will not be tried again tomorrow by some thug. What you will read and learn in the following pages, happens. People are knocked to the ground. People are kicked senseless on the streets.

I have seen so many victims in court, who, if only they knew how to effectively protect themselves and to grapple once on the ground, could have saved themselves a beating. If you end up on the ground on the street it is a whole lot different to a competition arena. You will need to know tactics and techniques within this text to save yourself a trip to hospital or worse!

Read this book. What you will learn from it is 'reality' of the streets and how to survive.

Matthew Adkins, Solicitor, 1999

The latest book by Jamie O'Keefe
NEW BREED PUBLISHING £14 inc P&P
PO BOX 511, DAGENHAM, ESSEX RM9 5DN

NO ONE FEARS
WHEN ANGRY!
The Psychology of
CONFRONTATION

Roy 'Pretty Boy' Shaw
And
Jamie O'Keefe
(Photo taken from book)

£ 14 inclusive of P&P
NEW BREED PUBLISHING   £14 inc P&P
PO BOX 511, DAGENHAM, ESSEX RM9 5DN

The new book by Alan Charlton

Awareness
Fears
And
Consequences

An insight to understanding what
you
can do to stay safe.
You may have only one chance and
only one choice

By Alan Charlton

NEW BREED PUBLISHING £14 inc P&P
PO BOX 511, DAGENHAM, ESSEX RM9 5DN

Forward
By
Darrin Richardson B.Sc. CMS

I have known Alan Charlton for many years, I have trained with him taught and been taught by him. He is undoubtedly one of the jewels in the art of self-protection in the United Kingdom. In well over 28 years I have seen many instructors, not all can live up to their reputation. Alan however is one. He has trained with some very notable instructors learning his art and developing his own approach to the subject matter. He like many of his kind did not wake up one day an expert instructor, practitioner and author, His skills have developed over many years, and some two years ago he decided to write down many of the lessons he has learnt.

In today's society we live with the fact that we may at anytime be exposed to some sort of violence. This is not just a statement to scare you it is an every day occurrence; all you need to do is open your local paper or watch your local news. It's out there for all to see, just staring you right in the face.

Awareness, fears and Consequences are your Highway Code. We all read the Highway Code before we take our driving tests; we don't remember it all (well I don't) but we do remember the basics. It is those basics that help us drive round in relative safety.

It's the same with Self-protection; Alan Charlton has waded through all the unnecessary ideas and skills that have become the myth of the martial arts and self-defence. We the reader can quickly learn many valuable lessons from this book, without the pain of having first hand experience. This book is crammed full of information and humour and is a must for the library of those who take the subject seriously.

Darrin Richardson 4th Dan

Please feel free to review any of our books on

www.amazon.co.uk

Why not also look at the dedicated websites of the
New Breed Authors

Jamie O'Keefe
www.newbreedbooks.co.uk

Kevin O'Hagan
www.bristolgoshinjutsu.com

Alan Charlton
www.spa.ukf.net

Steve Richards
www.renaissance-academy.com

Steve Richards

The latest author to join
Jamie O'Keefe
Kevin O'Hagan
& Alan Charlton
at New Breed Publishing

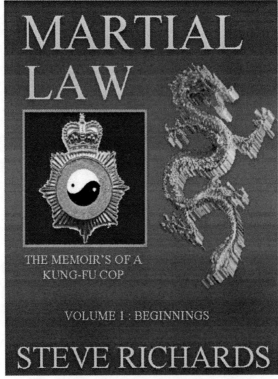

The memoirs of a Kung Fu cop
Part One – Beginnings

Topics include death, sex, serious injury, romance, pathos, tragedy, humour, riots, IRA, drugs, bouncers, getting planted and just about everything you'd expect from a Scouse Copper over 13 years front line duty. Also, loads on traditional Chinese arts from within their closed shop community, and how they worked or otherwise under real pressure. The post-police part of the book covers his martial arts and other careers since that time

£14 inclusive of P&P Available from
New Breed, Po box 511, Dagenham, Essex RM9 5DN

Coming soon

The memoirs of a Kung Fu cop
Part Two – Toxteth

£14 inclusive of P&P
Available soon from
New Breed soon
Po box 511, Dagenham, Essex RM9 5DN

Also coming soon
By Steve Richards
WARRIOR MIND
The Psychology of the Martial Arts

COMBAT

PANKRATION

Martial Art of the West

STEVE RICHARDS

Customer Info!

For Credit card orders please buy you books via

www.amazon.co.uk

Amazon will also take international orders.

To order by Cheque or Postal order

Please order direct from the relevant author or from
NEW BREED PUBLISHING
Po box 511
Dagenham
Essex RM9 5DN

If you order direct from author you can also get
them to include a personalised message and sign
the book!